Women Saints' Lives in
Old English Prose

Library of Medieval Women   ISSN 1369–9652

Series Editor: Jane Chance

Already published

Christine de Pizan's Letter of Othea to Hector, *Jane Chance*, 1990

The Writings of Margaret of Oingt, Medieval Prioress and Mystic, *Renate Blumenfeld-Kosinski*, 1990

Saint Bride and her Book: Birgitta of Sweden's Revelations, *Julia Bolton Holloway*, 1992

The Memoirs of Helene Kottanner (1439–1440), *Maya Bijvoet Williamson*, 1998

The Writings of Teresa de Cartagena, *Dayle Seidenspinner-Núñez*, 1998

Julian of Norwich: *Revelations of Divine Love* and *The Motherhood of God*, *Frances Beer*, 1998

Hrotsvit of Gandersheim: A Florilegium of her Works, *Katharina M. Wilson*, 1998

Hildegard of Bingen: On Natural Philosophy and Medicine: Selections from *Cause et cure, Margret Berger*, 1999

Women Saints' Lives in Old English Prose

**Translated from Old English
with Introduction, Notes and Interpretive Essay**

Leslie A. Donovan
University of New Mexico

D.S. BREWER

First published 1999
D. S. Brewer, Cambridge

ISBN 0 85991 568 9

D. S. Brewer is an imprint of Boydell & Brewer Ltd
PO Box 9, Woodbridge, Suffolk IP12 3DF, UK
and of Boydell & Brewer Inc.
PO Box 41026, Rochester, NY 14604–4126, USA
website: http://www.boydell.co.uk

A catalogue record for this book is available
from the British Library

Library of Congress Cataloging-in-Publication Data
Women saints lives in Old English prose / translated from Old English
   with introduction, notes, and interpretive essay, Leslie A. Donovan.
      p.   cm. – (Library of medieval women, ISSN 1369-9652)
   Includes bibliographical references (p.   ) and index.
   ISBN 0-85991-568-9 (pbk : alk. paper)
   1. Christian women saints Biography Early works to 1800.
   2. Christian literature, English (Old)   I. Donovan, Leslie A.,
   1957–   . II. Series.
   BX4656.W65   2000
   270.2′092′2 – dc21   99-40572

This publication is printed on acid-free paper

Printed in Great Britain by
Athenæum Press, Gateshead, Tyne & Wear

Contents

Introduction

> ... more glorious [is] the victory of those shown triumphing, espe-
> cially when womanly frailty emerges victorious, and virile force,
> confounded, is laid low.
>
> Hrotsvitha (c.935–1000)[1]

For tenth-century women like Hrotsvitha, the heroic strength of
spirit of women saints was a source of personal and public
inspiration to medieval women. This volume, unlike the other works
in the Library of Medieval Women series that translate the words of
medieval women themselves, presents the holy biographies or lives
of eight women saints: Æthelthryth, Agatha, Agnes, Cecilia, Eugenia,
Euphrosyne, Lucy, and Mary of Egypt. As one recent scholar
explains, women saints' lives such as these provide their audiences
with "sources of inspiration, authority, and empowerment for women
by suggesting a variety of relevant role models and experiences for
them to admire, imitate, or to modify in order to fit their special
needs or situations."[2] The diversity of experiences represented by
these texts provides a range of spiritual and personal possibilities
both for their medieval audiences and for modern readers seeking to
understand women's roles in early medieval culture.

These eight texts, Old English versions of earlier legends primarily from Greek and Latin sources, offer their readers perspectives on
holy women from all extremes of life. Characteristic of the larger
genre of medieval women saints' lives, these texts record the Old
English prose versions of the legendary stories of women escaping
from unwanted marriages, communicating on an equal footing with
male relatives and other male authorities, acquiring better educa-
tions, living autonomously as hermits in the desert, and gaining political and social authority. In them, we learn the histories of young

---

[1] Peter Dronke, *Women Writers of the Middle Ages: A Critical Study of Texts from
Perpetua (†203) to Marguerite Porete (†1310)* (Cambridge: Cambridge University Press, 1984), p. 69.

[2] Jane Schulenburg Tibbetts, *Forgetful of their Sex: Female Sanctity and Society,
ca 500–1100* (Chicago: University of Chicago Press, 1998), p. 56.

women, like the 13-year-old Agnes, as well as old women, like 76-year-old Mary of Egypt. They come from locations as geographically separated as England and Egypt. Like Æthelthryth, some of these women were actual historical women, while others, like Lucy, may be completely fictional. Five of these saints were martyred and three died of illness or natural causes. In this group of typical saints, we recognize highly feminine women such as Agnes and Cecilia, as well as masculinized women, such as Eugenia and Euphrosyne. Among these women are virgins, prostitutes, and celibate married women. Although most are born of the noble classes, some like Æthelthryth are even queens who have worn many jeweled necklaces. Others, like Mary of Egypt, are paupers who own no clothes to cover their bodies. Some of them are highly educated, like Eugenia who knows Latin and Greek, but some, like Mary of Egypt, have never even learned their letters.

Yet, even as disparate as these women's lives seem on the surface, they are all united by a common devotion to their Christian faith and to God. Their belief in Christianity and their efforts to lead virtuous and chaste lives, as defined by the doctrines of their faith, make these eight women spiritual kindred. Despite differences in their backgrounds and experiences, their lives are also united by similar narrative patterns. These legendary lives describe characters who often seem almost interchangeable, and develop spiritual themes that are nearly identical. In addition, fictional though many narrative elements may be, these saints' lives are based largely on historical figures and record cultural information about early women. Such lives not only document the importance of spiritual faith to early Christian women, but they also offer testimony concerning how these women used their faith as a tool for empowerment. Whether real or not, the lives of these eight women offer meaning, not only for their subjects, but also for later medieval Christian women, who were meant to reflect on the stories of these saintly women. All these holy biographies represent genuine concerns medieval women had about their own bodies, their physical vulnerability, their power in the world, and over their own selves. These lives represent the choices women had to make for themselves as well as portray their personal and public struggles to lead lives of value in the sociopolitical culture of Western Europe which restricted women's lives. Their stories offer a multilayered vision of women that is both historical and personal, radical and hegemonic, political and spiritual. They represent not so much stories of actual sequential events, but rather stories that depict various approaches to salvation history.

This collection of women saints' lives translated from Old English prose presents eight texts whose perspectives focus plainly on the goal of salvation. The *Life of St Æthelthryth* relates the story of an Anglo-Saxon noblewoman who lived between 630–679. Although she was married twice for political reasons, her legend insists that she never consummated her marriages and remained a virgin throughout her life. She founded an important monastery at Ely in 672, where she served as abbess until her death. Next, the *Life of St Agatha* describes the tribulations of a devout third-century Sicilian woman, who had dedicated her life to Christ from childhood. After rejecting the advances of a noble suitor to maintain her virginity, Agatha is tortured in a variety of ways, including having one of her breasts cut off and then miraculously restored, before she is martyred for her faith. Set in the late third or early fourth century, the *Life of St Agnes* tells the story of a thirteen-year-old Roman girl. Because she considers Christ her bridegroom, Agnes rejects a powerful pagan suitor, who tortures and executes her for not giving up her Christian beliefs. The *Life of St Cecilia* presents the legend of an early third-century Roman woman, who longs for a life of chastity, but is nevertheless married against her will. In her bridal bed on her wedding night, she explains her faith and her vow of chastity to her husband so persuasively that he agrees not only to respect her beliefs, but also converts to Christianity and is later martyred for his faith. After her husband's martyrdom, Cecilia refuses to partake in pagan rites and is also executed. One of over eighty female transvestite or cross-dressing saints' lives found throughout medieval Europe, the *Life of St Eugenia* relates the legend of a third-century saint from Alexandria. Eugenia's life describes how she disguises herself as a man, to receive a better Christian education, and becomes abbot of a monastery. Her true identity is exposed at a trial in which she is accused of raping a woman whom she had healed. Later, Eugenia is martyred for her faith. Describing the story of another cross-dressing saint, the *Life of St Euphrosyne* presents the story of a young woman who escapes from an unwanted marriage by dressing as a eunuch and joining a monastery. Because of her beauty, even dressed as a eunuch, Euphrosyne lives isolated as a hermit within the monastery. When she dies, she is discovered to be a woman and her dead body restores the sight of a blind monk. Recording the story of a fourth-century Sicilian noblewoman, the *Life of St Lucy* also portrays the saint's rejection of a suitor and her subsequent tortures. Lucy is saved from defilement in a brothel and from fire before she is finally executed by a sword thrust through her throat. The last text translated here is the *Life of St Mary of Egypt*. This life tells the legend of a fifth-century prostitute from Alexandria, who is converted to Christianity in a miraculous event at the celebration of the Exaltation of the Holy Cross. Afterward, she lives as a hermit in the desert. Her legend is intertwined with the story of Zosimus, an extremely pious monk, who learns from Mary of Egypt about her life and redemption as well as about her more personal approach to piety.

The legends of these eight holy women were told in many versions throughout most parts of Europe and the Middle East during late antiquity and the Middle Ages. The saints' lives translated here, however, represent their earliest vernacular versions. In Old English, these versions are contained in a mid-eleventh-century Anglo-Saxon manuscript of works written in the late tenth century by Ælfric.[3] This manuscript preserves the earliest, most complete surviving texts of Ælfric's saints' lives. Apart from two texts included in this manuscript that present the combined lives of saintly married couples,[4] the eight texts translated here are the only texts about women saints in Ælfric's collection. Although four texts[5] in this manuscript were not written by Ælfric, the manuscript collection is commonly referred to as *Ælfric's Lives of Saints*.[6] Few other prose texts of women saints' lives survive in Old English,[7] but two significant early poetic women saints' lives in Old English are *Juliana* and *Elene*, written by Cynewulf in the ninth century. These eight women saints' lives have

---

[3] The mid-eleventh-century manuscript, which serves as the base manuscript for the translations presented in this volume, is London, British Library, Cotton, Julius E.vii.

[4] While the *Life of St Cecilia* is also technically the story of a saintly married couple (Cecilia and her husband Valerian), it differs from the *Life of St Julian and his Wife Basilissa* and the *Life of Sts Chrysanthus and Daria* in that Cecilia's life is commonly listed under her name, as her history, while the other two lives are normally listed under both names. I have excluded translations of Ælfric's other two couple saints from this collection for this reason.

[5] These are the lives of Eustace, the Seven Sleepers, Euphrosyne, and Mary of Egypt. The latter two are translated here.

[6] This title was used by Walter W. Skeat in his 1900 edition of this manuscript and has since become the standard title for the Old English source of these lives.

[7] The only other women saints' lives in Old English prose are those of Margaret, Mildrith, and Sexburg. Although no edition exists for the fragmentary text of Sexburg's life, excellent modern editions of the Old English legends of Margaret and Mildrith have been published. These are: Mary Clayton and Hugh Magennis, eds., *The Old English Lives of St Margaret*, Cambridge Studies in Anglo-Saxon England 9 (Cambridge: Cambridge University Press, 1994); and David W. Rollason, ed., *The Mildrith Legend: A Study in Early Medieval Hagiography* (Leicester: Leicester University Press, 1982).

not been edited or translated since Walter W. Skeat's 1900 text and, until now, have never been presented together as a group in a way that emphasizes their function and content for the lives of medieval women. Presenting these eight women saints' lives together focuses attention on the intrinsically female aspects of hagiography in Anglo-Saxon England.

Origin and development of saints' lives in late antiquity and the Middle Ages

Although the narratives of saints' lives originated in late antiquity, as a literary genre such texts were most important to the culture of the Middle Ages. With over a thousand texts surviving in medieval manuscripts written either in Latin or in vernacular versions, saints' lives were possibly the most popular literary genre of medieval Europe. These "bestsellers" of the Middle Ages afford modern readers insights into the variety, complexities, and contradictions of medieval culture. They interweave historical fact with religious folk-lore, exemplifying the dualities intrinsic to medieval life. By joining the real to the fictional, the sacred to the profane, and the mystical to the practical, saints' lives contextualize and explicate many of what modern readers consider the contradictions inherent in medieval thought and culture. Yet, these texts are not accurate reflections of historical truth. Rather, these highly fictionalized and heavily pat-terned accounts were intended to validate contemporary spiritual experience, but were "not transparent windows into the saints' lives, their society or even the spirituality of the age."[8]

Because of the multidisciplinary nature of saints' lives, the genre of hagiography, or sacred biography, is not easily definable nor clearly categorized. In fact, recent studies of saints' lives have gone beyond traditional examinations of the narrative *vitae, passiones* and *translationes* that commonly recorded the stories of the lives and miracles associated with saintly Christians. Contemporary scholars of hagiography explore not only these more traditional narrative forms of the lives of saints, but also examine such materials as liturgies, hymns, martyrologies, sanctorales, litanies, church dedica-tions, breviaries, sermons, prayers for special occasions, legal docu-ments from religious orders, and relics. Such materials establish

---

[8] Patrick Geary, "Saints, Scholars, and Society: The Elusive Goal" in *Saints: Studies in Hagiography*, Medieval & Renaissance Texts & Studies 141, ed. Sandro Sticca (Binghamton, NY: State University of New York Press, 1996), p. 10.

evidence concerning the development and dissemination of the cult of a particular saint or group of saints. However, the immense volume of such materials and the widespread propagation of various versions of saints' lives throughout Europe over the course of many centuries makes hagiography not so much a genre as it is a cultural tradition. While the narratives are constructed similarly, the individual texts of saints' lives differ in focus or cultural meaning, depending on the geographical origin, intended audience, historical period, and sociopolitical conditions of the culture. Because of this, it becomes impossible to discover any general or common meaning of the *Life of St Agatha*, for example. Instead, we can only study what the *Life of St Agatha* might have meant to aristocratic Roman Christian audiences of the fifth century, to monks in ninth-century Carolingian monastic communities, or to laypeople in tenth-century Anglo-Saxon England.

In addition, what any one hagiographic text might have meant to any particular audience is at least partly dependent on what its author intended. In the case of saints' lives, however, authorship is more often a matter of adaptation of and accretion from earlier sources than it is the product of any singularly inspired mind. Little factual information remains concerning the writers from late antiquity who were responsible for composing the original Greek or Latin versions of the early saints' lives. Although we have more information about hagiographers from later periods, the original sources for most early saints' lives, including seven of the eight lives[9] translated here, were written by anonymous writers. Even so, we can be reasonably certain that the original narratives of the lives of early saints, such as Agatha, Agnes, Cecilia, Eugenia, Euphrosyne, Lucy, and Mary of Egypt, were written by male monastics, educated according to classical Greek and Roman standards, during the fifth through seventh centuries. While female or lay authorship cannot be completely ruled out for the earliest versions of such texts, the fact that Christian teaching and literature was predominantly controlled by male monastics at this time suggests male authorship. Further, while women certainly held positions of economic and political power during this time, their influence on the development of Christian literature would have been unusual enough for later redactors to have remarked upon original female authorship of such texts. Between 500 and 1100, few texts involving women saints are recorded to have

---

9   The early eighth-century *Life of St Æthelthryth* is the only text in this collection for which we know anything substantial about its original author, Bede.

been written by women. The reason so few women from this period wrote narrative biographies that had impact on their cultures is probably "not a reflection of the general level of their literary skill; rather, even if female religious did not believe that an abbess worthy of commemoration was, by definition, one whose Life was written by a man, interest in the Lives written by women was insufficient to generate enough copies to ensure their survival."[10]

Regardless of the original authorship of these early saints' lives, incipient knowledge of these holy legends apparently circulated widely throughout Europe and the Middle East during the second through fourth centuries. By the second century, public veneration of saints was common practice. Such veneration was based largely on the saint's tomb, at which miracles were said to have occurred, and on the occasion of the saint's death, at which time a holy feast was held in honor of the saint. This worship of the saint was a result of the belief of early Christians that "a martyr who shed his blood for Christ was certainly in Heaven and able to exercise intercessory prayer on behalf of those who invoked him."[11] In the early periods, holy individuals became considered saints largely by public acclaim within a specific, local Christian community. Normally, this honor was reserved for a Christian who "had either suffered death in persecution or been of such outstanding holiness that none could doubt of his eternal destiny."[12] Miracles, specifically those in which individuals were healed from illness or disease, were considered proof of the saint's sanctity. During the fourth and fifth centuries, devotion to the cults of saints became so widespread in Western Europe, as well as in the Eastern church, that even holy confessors and non-martyred virgins came to be considered saints. For these types of saints, "the ascetic, monastic life came to be regarded as something of a substitute for martyrdom, and those who pursued it faithfully as worthy of the same honour."[13] Not until the twelfth century was papal authority deemed necessary for determining sainthood. Since that time, the methods for canonizing saints have been reformed, but most of the early saints, including those translated for this collection, have retained their saintly status

---

[10] Stephanie Hollis, *Anglo-Saxon Women and the Church: Sharing a Common Fate* (Woodbridge: Boydell Press, 1992), p. 274.

[11] David Hugh Farmer, *Oxford Dictionary of Saints* (Oxford: Oxford University Press,1987), p. x.

[12] Farmer, *Oxford Dictionary of Saints*, p. xix.

[13] Farmer, *Oxford Dictionary of Saints*, p. xix.

because of the influence of their cults on early Christian history and culture.

In late antiquity or the early Christian era, a period in which Christians perceived themselves as engaged in a spiritual battle against pagan beliefs, stories about the early saints served to encourage believers and to support them in their efforts to reject social customs and political authority contradictory to their faith. These stories were intended primarily for those who already believed in Christian teachings, not for the unconverted. Once Christianity had become a powerful, though not yet completely dominant, social and political force in early medieval Western Europe, fully developed biographies of the saints grew in popularity. Such narratives were not biographies in the sense of relating events of the saint's life from beginning to end. Instead, as Alexandra Hennessey Olsen explains, "Hagiographic narratives combine biographical details with a polemical purpose."[14]

These saints' lives were used for a variety of religious purposes, including readings from them on the saints' feast days as part of the liturgical calendar. Although such lives were less necessary to bolster the resolution of Christian believers to maintain their faith against adversarial social elements than they had been in the early Christian era, narratives about holy men and women were increasingly necessary to validate the teachings and philosophies of Christian thinkers. It was these thinkers who influenced the evolution and predominance of this previously radical religious sect within the cultural environments of medieval Europe. As part of the growth of the faith, the early saints' lives were written with the express intention of illustrating Christian thought and doctrine by means of narrative exemplars. Although they were initially propagated among monastic communities in Europe and the Middle East, these texts rapidly also became popular texts by which monks and abbots attracted laypeople, especially from the noble classes, to the Christian faith. Because they were stories about idealized people, usually in extreme situations, such fully developed narratives possessed an entertainment value that monastic and clerical communities appropriated to increase their flocks of Christian followers.

Further, these saints' lives were meant as teaching devices, not so much to provide exemplars of behavior to be emulated by individual Christians, but to edify the faithful about salvation's history and future. In this way, these biographies were employed to support and

---

[14] Alexandra Hennessey Olsen, " 'De Historiis Sanctorum': A Generic Study of Hagiography," *Genre* 13 (Winter 1980): 415.

encourage existing Christians as well as to promote the faith to unbelievers or to those ambivalent in their beliefs.

Thus, from the beginning, saints' lives have been intentionally propagandistic. Just as they reflected profound spiritual truths, they also sometimes manipulated those truths to generate monastic propaganda to encourage economic support for advancing the causes and ideology of the Christian faith. In addition, as the Middle Ages progressed, many of these texts were also used to attract wealthy patrons to specific monastic communities.[15] The holy biographies of Eugenia, Euphrosyne, and Agatha served as advertisements for their monasteries or cities. These texts both encouraged attention from people in the region and inspired visits from people who lived far away. Significantly, those who first composed these holy biographies were not usually the people who used saints' lives for these purposes. Instead, most of the original texts came to be revised for specific audiences, copied numerous times, and then disseminated widely among Christian communities. Unlike modern texts whose original authorship is inseparable from the text itself, saints' lives were considered basically community property to be adapted for whatever purposes best suited the needs of the time and place. The concept of plagiarism was non-existent. Since these narratives were no single person's property, they were viewed as part of a Christian literary treasure-trove, which rightfully belonged to all the faithful and could be used to promote and glorify the faith as any Christian saw fit. In fact, saints' lives in the early Middle Ages were so systematically and consciously conceived as propaganda that they were "not simply reflective but programmatic. The production of hagiography, that is, not only the authoring of texts but also their copying and dissemination, was intentional action, even if its consequences, the uses to which these texts were put, were not intended by the producers."[16] Thus, saints' lives became products not so much of a single mind, but of a multitude of minds working toward the same aim, to glorify God and, in so doing, to enhance devotion by increasing the numbers of the faithful.

By the end of the sixth century, when most of the early saints' lives translated here had been written and widely disseminated, Christianity

---

[15] Although many have remarked on the propagandist nature of saints' lives, Aron Gurevich in *Medieval Popular Culture: Problems of Belief and Perception*, trans. Janós M. Bak and Paula M. Hollingsworth (Cambridge: Cambridge University Press, 1988) discusses this concept at some length.

[16] Patrick Geary, "Saints, Scholars, and Society: The Elusive Goal" in *Saints: Studies in Hagiography*, ed. Sandro Sticca, Medieval & Renaissance Texts & Studies 141 (Binghamton, NY: State University of New York Press, 1996), p. 15.

10 *Introduction*

had become formidably entrenched in Western European culture. At this time, the production of new medieval saints' lives begins to occur alongside continuing redactions of the earlier saints' lives. This production of both new and ancient saints' lives witnesses a refinement in the purpose and uses of earlier texts. While the stories of later saints were still presented using the same formulaic conventions and narrative structures characteristic of the earlier lives, medieval writers rarely needed new saints' lives for the purposes of conversion. Rather, as the Middle Ages progressed, later redactions of the early saints' lives included fewer specifics from the original stories and a greater focus on their spiritual themes. Although it is unlikely that even the earliest writers of holy biographies expected anyone in their audience actually to emulate the behavior of these early saints, during the Middle Ages it is more and more apparent that saints' lives were tributes to God's glory and that their subjects were meant to be venerated, admired, celebrated, and even learned from, but not to be imitated. The extremist, even revolutionary and sometimes antisocial, behavior of most of these early saints was conduct Christian authorities would have not considered conducive to the harmonious integration of Christian principles into medieval society and culture. Intended to display the glory of God working within the lives of idealized individuals, saints' lives were not expected to "provide models for mortals."[17]

In fact, in most cases, the saintly subjects of the early holy biographies were idealized figures, superior in every way to the average Christian in the Middle Ages. With a few notable exceptions,[18] the personal history of the saints embodies the noblest ideals of the culture. Depicting the saints as the paragons of sanctity,[19] these stories describe them as nobly born, exceedingly wise, extremely beautiful in appearance, steadfastly courageous, securely confident, and unswerving in devotion to their faith. As typified by the lives translated here, women saints never doubt their God and never exhibit any fear, even when facing the most horrible tortures. Perfect in faith, wisdom, heritage, and the force of their individual wills, they are heroes in the epic of salvation. Although human by birth and in form, they are presented as superhuman in virtue and faith. In this way, the saints themselves mediate between the human and the divine or, as one notable scholar has summarized, they join Earth and

---

[17] Patrick Geary, "Saints, Scholars, and Society," p. 15.
[18] Mary of Egypt translated here is an exception.
[19] Patrick Geary, "Saints, Scholars, and Society," p. 15.

Heaven.[20] But, such conventions are restricted not only to the portrayal of the saintly character; the rhetorical structures of saints' lives reflect formulaic narrative approaches as well. As the texts in this collection illustrate, saints' lives were commonly associated with each other through literary motifs, presentation of speeches, description of tortures and miracles, and biblical allusions. These texts borrow heavily from each other, from biblical sources, and from other religious authorities. Because of their insistence on a common vocabulary, descriptive imagery, religious themes, narrative patterns, and character paradigms, saints' lives are emphatically intertextual. They rely on each other and on a larger Christian cultural history to construct meaning.

Although it is easy for contemporary readers to interpret the referential qualities of such texts as repetitious and unoriginal, medieval audiences and readers apparently found these elements enormously satisfying. The substantial material resources expended to reproduce the vast number of surviving early saints' lives provide undeniable testimony that saints' lives were immensely popular with medieval audiences and significant to the development of a cohesive medieval religious culture. Indeed, however interchangeable these texts might seem to modern readers, from the earliest records of saints in late antiquity through the multitude of complete versions of legends disseminated throughout Europe by the end of the eleventh century, it is clear that early audiences appreciated texts that constantly reconsidered the same topics and themes with only slight variances in their external trappings. Creative distinctiveness was unimportant because, as one scholar notes, after audiences had heard the same story recited year after year on the saint's feast day, "originality would lose its point."[21] Embedded in the formulaic conventions and stereotypical characters of these texts, individual secular Christians, church authorities, and monastic caretakers discovered ways to understand the function of their ordinary lives within the larger scope of their extraordinary Christian heritage as illustrated by the saints' lives.

Traditions and conventions of women saints' lives

The lives of women saints were a means by which the medieval church sought to shape popular understanding of women's roles

20 Peter Brown, *The Cult of Saints* (Chicago: University of Chicago Press, 1981), p. 4.
21 Charles W. Jones, *Saints' Lives and Chronicles in Early England* (Ithaca, NY: Cornell University Press, 1947), p. 73.

within Christian culture. The facts of women's lives encoded in these texts provide evidence for understanding the history of women in Christianity, medieval religious thought, and medieval popular culture, as well as the development of women's spirituality. Written initially by writers of late antiquity and then adapted to suit the purposes of medieval redactors, they reflect the behavior of early women saints; they also reflect a later medieval society's response to these women along with a religious desire to reconstruct these women's experiences for Christianity's own purposes. These overlapping perspectives provide a valuable complement to the singular focus of works by individual medieval women. Framed quite differently from works by medieval women themselves, women saints' lives establish an understanding both of religious views about women and of the cultural environments in which medieval women actually lived. Where texts written by women offer insight into the creativity, inspiration, and motivation of individual medieval women, saints' lives about women present the personal histories of historical women as well as of the cultural and popular legacies such lives gave to later generations of medieval women. Conceiving these saints' lives as a vital part of their Christian heritage, many later medieval women[22] sought religious authorization of their own experiences in the legends of earlier women saints. In this way, these texts forged profound cultural and literary links between the historical Christians on which they may have been based, the medieval religious consciousness grappling with the implications of the legends of such women, and the later medieval women who looked to these stories for confirmation and validation of their own lives.

During late antiquity and the Middle Ages, the pursuit of sanctity clearly promoted different paths for men and women. Using statistical analyses of 864 saints, Weinstein and Bell present evidence that throughout this period, veneration of saints "continued to be sex-differentiated," with women saints representing only 17.5 percent of their sample.[23] Nevertheless, although it cannot be denied that more male saints' lives survive than female saints' lives, the legends of holy women also attracted significant religious interest. From the earliest development of the cults of saints, women were commonly

---

[22] See, for example, the writings of Margery Kempe, an English mystic of the late fourteenth and early fifteenth century.

[23] Donald Weinstein and Rudolph M. Bell, *Saints and Society: The Two Worlds of Western Christendom, 1000–1700* (Chicago: University of Chicago Press, 1982), p. 220.

venerated. Collections of saints' lives from the Middle Ages almost always present the holy biographies of both men and women, suggesting that their compilers saw no reason to distinguish certain texts for specific audiences. As Caroline Bynum notes, "Both men and women saw female saints as models of suffering and inner spirituality."[24] Yet, while it is evident that early and medieval Christians considered both women and men as deserving honor for their sanctity, women saints' lives held a different appeal for medieval male and female audiences. It is likely that male audiences, often composed of secluded, celibate male monastics, may have focused on the otherness of sexual dangerousness of the female saint. In contrast, female audiences may have recognized the tensions between the physical and spiritual in women saints' lives as mirroring their own struggles.

In addition to differences between central experiences for different audiences, the narrative patterns also reveal a differing goal of men and women's saints' lives. For example, although chastity was required of both male and female saints, its practice for women saints was represented as the individual's desire for spiritual purity as well as the result of a woman's special status as the bride of Christ.[25] These holy biographies not only highlight the woman saint's fidelity to her divine bridegroom, but also foreground the resolution with which she maintains that fidelity. For the woman saint, her role as the spouse of Christ was not only her confirmed duty within the design of the sacred biography, but more important, her divine betrothal was a privilege to be zealously defended.[26]

Together with the hagiographic requirement that female saints' lives differ from male saints' lives in that their subjects remain virginal for such a specialized reason, the heroic actions of male and female saints offer opposing constructs. The male saint generally achieves his spiritual heroism either by resisting sexual temptation or

---

[24] Caroline Walker Bynum, *Holy Feast and Holy Fast: The Religious Significance of Food to Medieval Women* (Berkeley: University of California Press, 1987), p. 25.

[25] Although concerned primarily with women saints from France, many of the remarks Karl D. Uitti makes in his article "Women Saints, the Vernacular, and History in Early Medieval France" pertain to this concept. This article appears in *Images of Sainthood in Medieval Europe*, ed. Renate Blumenfeld-Kosinski and Timea Szell (Ithaca, NY: Cornell University Press, 1991), pp. 247–67.

[26] A more detailed discussion of hagiographic issues of specific importance in women saints' lives may be found in Thomas J. Heffernan's *Sacred Biography: Saints and their Biographers in the Middle Ages* (Oxford: Oxford University Press, 1988).

by refusing to abandon his faith. In contrast, women saints' lives show their subjects heroically preserving their virginity against physical assault from male antagonists. Describing this pattern, Elizabeth Robertson writes,

> In most male saints' lives, where sexual temptation might be one problem for the male contemplative, it was subordinated in a progressive series of temptations, usually culminating in a temptation to pride. In female saints' lives, sexual tempta- tion was either the saints' sole or her central temptation.[27]

Yet, such sexual temptation is normally presented as a one-sided activity in female saints' lives. At least in the saints' lives translated for this volume, the women themselves never exhibit any signs of being tempted by their would-be sexual partners. Rather, it is the pagan male adversary who is tempted by the woman saint's physical beauty and her denied sexuality. His physical assault on the woman saint's virginity is often violent, as in the case of Agatha, translated here, whose breast is cut off when she refuses to submit sexually to her pagan suitor. In other cases, the masculine assault on the woman saint is mental as well as physical. The lives of Agatha and Lucy, for example, present stories in which men attempt to compel the woman saint to acquire knowledge of sexual seductions. In an effort to subvert the saints' chastity, the suitors in these stories attempt to force these saints to learn the practices of sinful sexuality from pros- titutes. The woman saint's resolute refusal to consider or bow to these practices is her defense from such mental assault.

By denying their female sexuality, which would normally have been reserved for their husbands, women saints also become cultural rebels. During both late antiquity and the early Middle Ages, women led lives largely confined and controlled by male authorities and family members. While many exceptional women accomplished impressive feats or led extraordinary lives, these were generally the exceptions to society's rules. Women saints were exceptional, not only in their faith, but also in their rejection of the circumscribed options for female fulfillment. They are "transgressors," to use Elizabeth Alvilda Petroff's words.[28] However, this transgressive

---

[27] Elizabeth Robertson, *Early English Devotional Prose and the Female Audience* (Knoxville: University of Tennessee Press, 1990), p. 40.

[28] Although writing about Italian women saints from a period later than that of the legends translated here, Petroff's "The Rhetoric of Transgression in the *Lives of Italian Women Saints*," in her book *Body and Soul: Essays on Medieval Women and Mysticism* (Oxford: Oxford University Press, 1994), offers a useful

conduct is not an exclusive trait of women saints for all early saints are transgressors,

> in the sense that a saint lives by excess, lives in a beyond where ordinary measure does not hold; all saints, by their lives, stretch the boundaries of what we have conceived of as human possibility, and their zeal in breaking through conventional limitations can be both attractive and repellent, pointlessly mad and unshakeably sane at the same time.[29]

Even so, women saints become "doubly transgressors," because they not only reflect the cultural transgressions of most saints described above, but also because they transgress against their nature as women.[30] The women subjects of the saints' lives translated here breach marriage customs, sexual responsibilities, familial authority, and political status. Most of all, they insist on the supremacy of their own will as a vehicle of their faith and, in so doing, make themselves objects of public regard and controversy. Puzzling though veneration of such female transgressors may seem in light of the misogynistic tendencies of medieval culture, the fact that medieval writers continued to preserve and adapt these stories of ancient women for their own audiences and purposes suggests that this transgressive legacy was too intrinsic to the history of female sanctity to be suppressed.

Religious background for saints' lives in Anglo-Saxon England

Although Christianity was known in Britain from as early as the fourth century, the official conversion of Anglo-Saxon England to Roman Christianity began in 597, when St Augustine of Canterbury was sent on a mission to England by St Gregory (c.540–604). Despite some early conflicts between Roman and Celtic Christianity, during the next several centuries the expression of religious thought in Britain took much of its content, attitudes, and style from continental models and influences. Yet, while members of British religious communities were heavily influenced by their peers on the continent, their own work had significant impact on religious communities outside of England. English writers such as Bede and Aldhelm in the seventh and eighth centuries wrote works that were praised and studied by their contemporaries and by later religious authorities in

interpretation of the transgressive nature of women saints that is applicable to the subject of this collection.

[29] Elizabeth Alvilda Petroff, "The Rhetoric of Transgression," p. 161.
[30] Elizabeth Alvilda Petroff, "The Rhetoric of Transgression," p. 161.

Western Europe.[31] Such Anglo-Latin writers were largely responsible for the dissemination of and interest in the cults of early saints
in Anglo-Saxon England. Although heroic elements were crucial to
the appeal of saints' lives from the inception of the genre in late
antiquity, the emphasis on saint as hero was especially emphasized
in stories of the early saints throughout the Anglo-Saxon period.
While the point should not be overstated, saints' lives provided a
means for promoting God's power as sovereign over the pagan gods
in Anglo-Saxon culture no less than over pagan gods in late antique
Mediterranean cultures. As one scholar explains, "if the Anglo-Saxon
church was to confront paganism with any degree of success, it had
to demonstrate power superior to that which it challenged. Saints'
lives had their part to play in reinforcing this message."[32] To this end,
Anglo-Saxon and Anglo-Latin writers adopted many elements of
the Germanic warrior-hero for use in their retellings of the saints'
lives.

By the tenth century, the Benedictine Revival, which originated on
the continent, had spread to England and was influencing Anglo-
Saxon religious communities and the organization of religious
authority. The Benedictine Revival, which continued into the eleventh century, produced many of the most important literary, artistic,
and cultural works from Anglo-Saxon England. Especially important
in the reformation and reorganization of English religious communities at this time was Æthelwold, bishop of Winchester.[33] In keeping
with the Benedictine reforms in continental monasteries, Æthelwold
instituted many monastic reforms and was instrumental to the revival
of scholastic learning and literature in England during the tenth
century. Largely under Æthelwold's direction, the language of
literary production became more standardized and the West Saxon
dialect became the predominant form for the development of late
Anglo-Saxon literature.[34] Æthelwold was an important figure, not
only because of his impact on religious culture and learning in
tenth-century Anglo-Saxon England, but also because he influenced

---

[31] Bede's *History of the English Church and its People* and Aldhelm's *Carmen de
Virginitate.*

[32] Dee Dyas, *Images of Faith in English Literature 700–1500: An Introduction*
(London: Longman, 1997), p. 65.

[33] Æthelwold was made bishop of Winchester in c.963.

[34] For more information, see Helmut Gneuss' article "The Origin and Standard Old
English at Æthelwold's School at Winchester," *Anglo-Saxon England* 1 (1972):
63–83.

many of the most important writers of the late tenth century, including Ælfric.

One of Æthelwold's pupils and the bishop of Eynsham, Ælfric lived c.955–1020. He has been called "the greatest scholar of the English Benedictine revival,"[35] "the most distinguished intellectual monk of his generation,"[36] and "the first major writer of English prose."[37] Ælfric was particularly concerned with teaching appropriate responses and attitudes toward Christian doctrine to his fellow-monks as well as to pious laypeople. His efforts as a teacher are reflected in his writings, which display a concern that "his instruction should be easily intelligible and unquestionably orthodox."[38] Written near the close of the tenth century, Ælfric's *Lives of Saints*, as well as his two volumes of the *Catholic Homilies*, indicate his desire to balance the needs of his audience and the requirements of his monastic obligations. While some have perceived Ælfric's influence on his culture as being that of an adaptor or translator, rather than an original thinker, it is more accurate to consider Ælfric, as Barbara Raw does, "a theologian in his own right, whose writings form an important link between those of the Carolingian period and the theological works of the late eleventh and early twelfth centuries."[39] Despite careful attention to his Latin sources, Ælfric is equally attentive to his own culture's heritage as proven by his unique efforts to write his saints' lives in a rhythmical prose style[40] indebted to Germanic alliterative poetry. He also treats his Latin sources with a freedom that would be uncharacteristic of a simple redactor, in that he "omits, condenses, expands, rearranges, synthesizes two or more interpretations, rejects one in favour of another, imports examples or parallel texts, reminds us of something he has dealt with more extensively elsewhere."[41]

---

35 Dee Dyas, *Images of Faith in English Literature*, p. 270.
36 Eric John, *Reassessing Anglo-Saxon England* (Manchester: Manchester University Press, 1996), p. 127.
37 James Hurt, *Ælfric* (New York: Twayne Publishers, 1972), pp. 136–37.
38 Dee Dyas, *Images of Faith in English Literature*, p. 92.
39 Barbara Raw, *Trinity and Incarnation in Anglo-Saxon Art and Thought*, Cambridge Studies in Anglo-Saxon England 21 (Cambridge: Cambridge University Press), p. 3.
40 While there has been some debate over whether Ælfric's works should be considered prose or poetry, most contemporary scholars agree that his writing style is best described as prose highlighted by rhythmical alliterative accents.
41 J.C. Pope, *Homilies of Ælfric: A Supplementary Collection*, vol. I, Early English Text Society Original Series 259 (London: Early English Text Society, 1967–68), p. 150.

Like his other works, Ælfric's *Lives of Saints*,[42] from which the lives collected here are translated, was founded on his perception that proper instruction in Christian principles was seriously lacking among his contemporaries. With many of his contemporaries, Ælfric was convinced that teaching such principles in texts like the *Lives of Saints* was especially important, since the end of the first millennium heralded an impending Judgment Day. As Ælfric himself describes this need in his Preface to the *Catholic Homilies I*: "men particularly require good teaching in this age which is the end of the world."[43] As he states in the Latin opening of his Preface to the *Lives of Saints*, Ælfric envisioned his audience to be chiefly laypeople who would gain spiritual benefit to "revive a failing faith"[44] from learning about saints of particular importance to monastic communities. In his Old English Preface to the *Lives of Saints*, Ælfric gives us additional information about the purpose and intended audience for his text. He specifically names two ealdormen, Æthelweard and Æthelmær, as motivating his decision to write saints' lives in the Old English language. As Ælfric writes:

> I have now gathered in this book those Passions of the Saints as I have had space to translate into English, because you, dear [Æthelweard], and Æthelmær earnestly begged me for such compositions, and have received them from my hands as confirmation of your belief, because of this history that you have never before had in your language.

Both Æthelweard and Æthelmær were noble laymen, who apparently had some education and had been patrons of Ælfric. Since the ninth century, English laypeople had been educated in monastic settings as well as by monks in secular environments. This established an audience of educated laypeople and their families for texts such as Ælfric's. In his Preface to the *Lives of Saints*, Ælfric suggests that

---

[42] Most of Ælfric's important literary works were written at the close of the tenth century, including the *Lives of Saints* text used here. Unfortunately, no manuscripts of Ælfric's original text survive. The manuscript used for the translations collected here, however, was copied within approximately fifty years of Ælfric's text. Although the manuscript includes works not written by Ælfric, its inclusion of Ælfric's Preface suggests a conscious intention to preserve his authorship of these texts and indicates that this manuscript was closely related to the original text.

[43] Dorothy Whitelock, ed., *English Historical Documents: c.500–1042*, 2nd edn (London: Eyre Methuen, 1979), p. 924.

[44] From Ælfric's Preface, as translated by Walter W. Skeat in *Ælfric's Lives of Saints* (London: Early English Text Society, 1881–1900; repr.1966), p. 3.

Æthelweard was able not only to read Old English, but probably also knew some Latin.

Yet, Ælfric clearly intended his collection of saints' lives to serve an audience larger than Æthelweard and Æthelmær. In fact, although he considers these two noblemen his primary patrons, Ælfric expects that his choice to translate the saints' lives into the vernacular language will allow many others access to his work. By choosing to render such texts into the vernacular Old English, Ælfric is making a radical departure from Christian tradition. Ælfric's Preface indicates that he is highly conscious of the risks of such a vernacular translation. That he expects criticism for his effort is obvious from his statement, "Let it not be considered as a fault in me that I turn sacred narrative into our own tongue, since the request of many of the faithful shall clear me in this matter."[45] While he is not the first writer to present religious themes or narratives in Old English, Ælfric is the first to translate the complete narrative accounts of these saints and collect them into a text for laypeople. His choice to do so obviously warrants some explanation, which he gives in the opening to his Latin Preface:

> This book also I have translated from the Latin into the usual
> English speech, desiring to profit others by edifying them in
> the faith whenever they read this relation, as many, namely,
> as are pleased to study this work, either by reading or hearing
> it read.[46]

Such a statement not only explains Ælfric's intentions, but it implies a lay audience whose educational experiences vary and whose knowledge of literacy may be based on either oral or written traditions. In its implication of multiple literary experiences, Ælfric's Preface invites us to consider the women, as well as the men, who may have been members of his audience.

Women in Anglo-Saxon religion and culture

From the earliest periods, women held positions of power and authority in Anglo-Saxon religious and secular communities.[47]

---

[45] From Ælfric's Latin Preface, as translated by Walter W. Skeat in *Ælfric's Lives of Saints*, p. 5.

[46] From Ælfric's Latin Preface, as translated by Walter W. Skeat in *Ælfric's Lives of Saints*, p. 3.

[47] Much has been written about women in Anglo-Saxon history and culture, but an exhaustive review of such scholarship falls outside the scope of this work. Some particularly useful works on this subject are: Jane Chance, *Woman as Hero in Old English Literature* (Syracuse, NY: Syracuse University Press, 1986); Helen

Anglo-Saxon women were queens who ruled equally with male rulers, led armies to battle, and built fortresses for the people's defense. They were also abbesses who advised men of power on the continent, founded monastic communities, and influenced the development of church policies. Like the eighth-century nun Leoba, many women were highly educated in Latin literature and wrote poetry or prose. Others, such as those in the community of nuns at Barking for whom Aldhelm wrote his treatise on virginity, were expected to be competent in at least the basics of Latin literary style, patristic texts, and church history. Even so, many women in Anglo-Saxon convents were probably unable to read or write, but had knowledge of religious and secular literature through oral traditions. This would have been most common among women from the lesser nobility.

Royal women wielded particular influence on the development of Anglo-Saxon religious culture. Not only were women born into royal families married to insure political and economic alliances, but many of them were also placed in religious communities to establish spiritual affiliations. Affiliations with spiritual authorities and with influential religious communities were often as valuable to royal families as secular confederations of power. As one recent scholar describes such practices:

> Anglo-Saxon kings who not only allowed but encouraged their female relatives to set up monastic communities were taking best advantage of available talent. The installation of royal women as monastic founders avoided the necessity of the use in the same role of male relatives, who were needed at the king's side, as part of the complex social structure of kinship and loyalties that held together the warband, the foundation of secular power. On the other hand, the role of royal abbesses as advisors, hostesses, and diplomats in many ways echoed that of their sisters in the secular world.[48]

With royal women as abbesses of religious communities, their

Damico and Alexandra Hennessey Olsen, eds., *New Readings on Women in Old English Literature* (Bloomington: Indiana University Press, 1990); Christine Fell, *Women in Anglo-Saxon England* (London: British Museum Publications, 1984); and Stephanie Hollis, *Anglo-Saxon Women and the Church: Sharing a Common Fate* (Woodbridge: Boydell Press, 1992).

[48] Carol Neuman de Vegvar, "Saints and Companions to Saints: Anglo-Saxon Royal Women Monastics in Context" in *Holy Men and Holy Women: Old English Prose Saints' Lives and their Contexts*, ed. Paul E. Szarmach (Albany: State University of New York Press, 1996), p. 54.

royal families gained significant advantages, including access to spiritual authority and influence. In return, the church acquired sponsorships for the training of its clergy in the region controlled by the royal family. The royal family was also expected to contribute financially to the maintenance and success of the religious community. The woman herself could gain access to advanced education, increased administrative opportunities, and freedom from secular marital obligations. Although life for a royal woman could certainly have been as restrictive in a religious environment as it was in secular society, monastic communities offered an alternative for women who were widows, who were the youngest of many daughters, who preferred celibacy, who had political ambitions, and who yearned for spiritual fulfillment.

Many of these royal Anglo-Saxon women were abbesses, as was Æthelthryth whose life is translated here, and governed double monasteries housing both men and women.[49] In fact, some of the most prominent double monasteries in Anglo-Saxon England were founded and governed by abbesses who were royal women.[50] Such double monasteries, modeled on Frankish institutions, were, in fact, generally governed by women, who possessed substantial control of their communities. For example, they had the authority to establish the rules and customs of their communities as long as these were consistent with general spiritual principles governing other monastic settings. In addition, they administered the spiritual priorities and devotional practices of their monasteries. The economic resources provided by royal patronage of these double monasteries frequently encouraged them to become important centers of learning and education. In this way, such royal abbesses were responsible for the education of many men who achieved positions of religious power. In one case, the highly influential monastery at Whitby, founded in the seventh century, trained six bishops during the abbess Hild's administration. Such royal abbesses played crucial roles in the "formation of the church through the training of clergy, but also taking an active role in contemporary events, often by presence at court and synods."[51]

The efforts of such royal women and their less noble sisters, who

---

[49] For a more detailed discussion of royal Anglo-Saxon abbesses, see Susan J. Ridyard's *Royal Saints of Anglo-Saxon England: A Study of West Saxon and East Anglian Cults* (Cambridge: Cambridge University Press, 1988).

[50] Among these are the monasteries at Whitby, Coldingham, Ely, Wimbourne, and Thanet.

[51] Carol Neuman de Vegvar, "Saints and Companions to Saints," p. 55.

also founded, lived, and worked in monasteries or convents, attest to
an early tradition of women as teachers and educated citizens in
Anglo-Saxon England. These women would certainly have been
familiar with the lives of women saints. Works by Aldhelm, Bede,
and from the *Old English Martyrology* confirm that the lives of the
eight women saints translated in this collection were important
sources of contemplation and devotion for religious women as well
as men. Yet, while we can assume that Ælfric would have expected
his *Lives of Saints* to circulate among religious communities, it is
important to remember that Ælfric himself acknowledges that his
primary audience for this text was the laity. The lay audience that
Ælfric describes as being both readers and listeners of his work
would have been represented not only by Æthelweard and Æthelmær,
but also by other members of their households. These other members
of their households would have included wives, mothers, and daughters, who may or may not have been able to read or write, but who
would have been part of a lay community guided by Ælfric's spiritual counsel. Thus, Ælfric's saints' lives, like those of many hagiographers of the early Middle Ages, were "directed toward a
monastic community and had special appeal and relevance to audiences of female religious, as well as noblewomen who followed a
life of monastic virtue within the confines of their home."[52]

Although this extended audience of Ælfric's includes women from
an impressive monastic heritage as well as laywomen associated
with spiritually-inclined noble households, it must not be ignored
that the *Lives of Saints* offers the narratives of only eight women
saints out of a total of twenty-seven saints' lives. Discouraging as
this may be to modern readers seeking strong images of women
within the Benedictine Revival, it undeniably reflects the culture and
background of both Ælfric and tenth-century Anglo-Saxon England.
As a male monk trained within an exclusively male monastic community, located in a region where women exercised less power than
in earlier times, Ælfric was a product of his society. Understandably,
his literary interests and experience were largely the result of his
work governing men at Eynsham and interacting with the secular
men whom he advised. What is important for the purposes of the
translations presented here is that, even in such an extremely patriarchal setting as Ælfric's, the lives of women saints were still studied,
valued, and honored.

[52] Jane Tibbetts Schulenburg, *Forgetful of their Sex: Female Sanctity and Society,
ca 500–1100* (Chicago: University of Chicago Press, 1998), p. 27.

The lives of Æthelthryth, Agatha, Agnes, Cecilia, Eugenia, Euphrosyne, Lucy, and Mary of Egypt continued to hold the interest of men and women in the Anglo-Saxon period as they did in late antiquity. While narratives of women's sanctity may have been less prevalent in tenth-century England than they were in fifth-century Italy and Greece, the histories of women not only survived, but were transformed from culture to culture and from time to time. These legends of women's bravery, conviction, and devotion meant something different to their different audiences. One can only imagine that what the cutting off of Agatha's breast meant to Æthelweard was probably very different from what it meant to Æthelweard's wife or to a nun at Barking who read the story out loud to her sisters on the saint's feast day. Just so, the lives of the women saints collected in this volume have a completely different meaning for students and scholars at the turn of the second millennium, who have knowledge of feminism and sexual abuse. These saints' lives offer us a continuum that links contemporary issues with medieval and ancient concerns. Theirs is a legacy of women's freedom as well as spiritual suffering. By studying the tenth-century versions of these particular women saints' lives, modern readers will gain not only a comprehensive understanding of ancient or Anglo-Saxon women, but will also discover a rich heritage of female identities and, perhaps, their own debt to the women whose cultures have shaped our own.

*

I wish to express my gratitude to some of the many colleagues, research assistants, friends, and family without whose help this collection would never have been accomplished. In particular, I wish to thank: the Research Allocations Committee at the University of New Mexico for financial assistance; Rosalie Otero and all my other colleagues in the University Honors Program at the University of New Mexico for mental support and willingness to temporarily relieve me of departmental obligations so I could finish this book; my tenure committee for their patience and efforts on my behalf; my students Steven Mexal, Sarah Peters, and Lorraine Pratt for invaluable research assistance; Helen Damico for her gracious feedback on this work and for her constant encouragement throughout the last seventeen years; Paul Remley for first leading me down the twisted path of hagiographic scholarship; my family of Donovans, Parkers, and Cinis for much support and assistance; and Jeanell Pelsor for editorial and research assistance as well as immense personal support.

Note to the Translations

I have translated the works in this collection to reflect the content and intention of the Old English texts as closely as possible. However, the Anglo-Saxon that produced these texts was used predominantly in an oral culture. Its grammar and syntax is frequently quite different from Modern English. Also, the recitative use of repetition does not translate well for audiences like ours who live in a literary culture. Although I have taken much care to maintain the literary intentions of the original texts, I have taken many liberties in translation in order to provide texts that satisfy the requirements of a reading culture. Those who need a literal translation for linguistic purposes should refer to Skeat's edition of *Ælfric's Lives of Saints*.

Some liberties in translation warrant particular mention. For example, when translation would obscure referents of pronouns, I have silently supplied proper nouns for clarification. I have also often substituted personal pronouns for definite or demonstrative articles to conform more closely to modern usage. In addition, I have omitted many conjunctions related to the sequence of events (most commonly *þā, þus,* and *and*), as well as frequently used rhetorical markers (such as *witodlīce* and *sōðlīce*), in order to avoid a repetitious quality that, however satisfying it may have been for Anglo-Saxon audiences, modern readers consider unnecessary and interruptive. All such emendations modify minor technical aspects of the language or prose style, but never the content of the text. Special emendations are always noted in the translation. In the case of personal and place names, I have regularized spelling to coincide with forms most commonly found in modern scholarship.

Throughout these texts, I have translated the Old English term *mæden* in its various forms as its Modern English cognate *maiden*, instead of the other possibility, *virgin*. While *virgin* would be more cognate with *virgo* used in the original Latin texts, the connotations of *virgin* for modern readers are so heavily sexualized, and in some cases slightly demeaning, that its use in these texts seemed potentially distracting to their overall intentions. Since, at its worst, the term *maiden* connotes only a slightly archaic quality, while retaining the appropriate denotations of chastity as well as female youth, I have preferred it over *virgin*.

Concerning the matter of Ælfric's rhythmical prose style, I have found it impossible to preserve alliterative features and render a text suitable for modern audiences. While Ælfric's frequent alliteration is poetically pleasing in its Old English form, it does not translate easily or clearly into the modern idiom. Therefore, I have chosen to forgo alliteration in favor of a translation more readable for modern audiences.

Abbreviations and Key to Latin Sources

Ado (Latin martyrology compiled by Ado, c.875):
Martyrologium cum Additatmentis, ed. Héribert Rosweyde, in PL 123:139–436.

Aldhelm (Latin poetry from Anglo-Saxon England, c.685–710):
Aldhelm: The Poetic Works, trans. James L. Rosier and Michael Lapidge (Cambridge: D.S. Brewer, 1985*)*.

AS:
Acta Martyrum et Sanctorum, ed. Paul Bedjan (Paris: Harrassowitz, 1890–97).

Bede's *History* (Latin prose history from Anglo-Saxon England, c.731):
The History of the English Church and its People, trans Leo Sherley-Price, rev. R.E. Latham (New York: Penguin Books, 1968).

Bede's *Martyrology* (early eighth-century Latin martyrology from Anglo-Saxon England):
Martyrologium. Édition pratique des Martyrologes de Béde, de l'Anonyme Lyonnais et de Florus, ed. Jacques Dubois and Geneviève Renaud (Paris: CNRS, 1976).

BHG:
Bibliotheca Hagiographica Graeca, François Halkin, ed. (Brussels: Société des Bollandistes, 1957).

BHL:
UCL Bibliotheca Hagiographica Latina Manuscripta, ed. Société des Bollandistes, Université Catholique de Louvain, 12 August 1998 <http://bhlms.fltr.ucl.ac.be/>.

Florus (Latin martyrology compiled by Florus of Lyons, c.837):
Martyrologium. Édition pratique des Martyrologes de Béde, de l'Anonyme Lyonnais et de Florus, ed. Jacques Dubois and Geneviève Renaud (Paris: CNRS, 1976).

Hieronymian (eighth-century Latin martyrology originally incorrectly attributed to St Jerome):
Martyrologium Hieronymianum, ed. J. de Rossi and L. Duchesne, *Acta Sanctorum Novembris* 2.1 (Brussels: Société des Bollandistes, 1894).

Hrabanus (Latin martyrology by Hrabanus Maurus, c.780–856):
  Martyrologium, ed. John McCulloh, *Corpus Christianorum. Continuatio Medievalis* 44 (Turnhout: Brepols, 1979).
Lyons (Anonymous Latin martyrology from Lyons, c.806):
  Martyrologium. Édition pratique des Martyrologes de Béde, de l'Anonyme Lyonnais et de Florus, ed. Jacques Dubois and Geneviève Renaud (Paris: CNRS, 1976).
MCR (Latin metrical calendar from Ramsey in Anglo-Saxon England, c.990):
  Michael Lapidge, "A Tenth-Century Metrical Calendar from Ramsey" in *Anglo-Latin Literature: 900–1066* (London: The Hambledon Press, 1993), pp. 343–87.
Mombrizio:
  Sanctuarium seu Vitae Sanctorum, ed. Boninus Mombrizio (Paris: Le Goff, 1910).
Notker (Latin martyrology compiled by Notker, c.912):
  Martyrologium in PL 131:1029–1164.
OEM (Late ninth-century anonymous Old English Martyrology):
  Der Altenglische Martyrologium, ed. Günter Kotzor (Munich: Bayerische Akademie der Wissenschaften, 1981).
PG:
  Patrologiae Cursus Completus: Series Graeca, ed., Jacques-Paul Migne (Paris: Garnieri Fratres, 1857–76).
PL:
  Patrologiae Cursus Completus: Series Latina, ed. Jacques-Paul Migne (Paris: Garnieri Fratres, 1844–91).
Usuard (Latin martyrology compiled by Usuard, c.838–75):
  Le Martyrologe d'Usuard: Texte et Commentaire, ed. Jacques Dubois, Subsidia Hagiographica 40 (Paris: Société des Bollandistes, 1965).
Wormald (Various religious calendars from Anglo-Saxon England):
  Francis Wormald, ed., *English Kalendars Before AD 1100*, Henry Bradshaw Society 72 (London: Henry Bradshaw Society, 1934).
Willibrord (Latin calendar compiled by St Willibrord, c.658–739):
  The Calendar of St Willibrord, Henry Bradshaw Society 55, ed. H.A. Wilson (London: Henry Bradshaw Society, 1918; reprinted, 1998).

Women Saints' Lives

Æthelthryth

Æthelthryth[1] is the earliest of the English women saints and the only native English saint in this collection. Also the most historically reliable account of any of the women presented here, Æthelthryth's legend presents the story of the daughter of an East Anglian king. She lived c.630–679 and was married twice for political reasons, the second time to the heir of the king of Northumbria. Her own family's influence as well as the alliances formed by her two marriages gave Æthelthryth the prominence through which she was able to accomplish her religious goals. In particular, a tract of land called Ely was her morning-gift from her first husband. It was on this land that Æthelthryth founded the important Anglo-Saxon double monastery[2] at Ely in c.672. By 1066, this monastery was one of the two wealthiest in England. Æthelthryth is categorized as a virgin saint, and her feast day is celebrated on June 23.

The holy biography of Æthelthryth is first told by Bede in the *History of the English Church and its People*,[3] written in 731. Bede tells his readers that he acquired his information about Æthelthryth directly from the same Wilfrid, bishop of Northumbria, who is mentioned in the text. Bede was so impressed with Æthelthryth's story that he also composed a poem in her honor.[4] A later poetic version of Æthelthryth's life was written by Gregory of Ely in c.1170.[5] A longer

---

[1] The saint's name may also be spelled as Etheldreda and is sometimes listed under Audrey, a later version of the same name.

[2] A monastery for both men and women, such monasteries are usually governed by an abbess in Anglo-Saxon England.

[3] The Latin text of Bede's *History* may be found in AS, June 4, pp. 489–582. BHL lists the Latin sources under items 2632–40. Bede tells Æthelthryth's story in book IV, chapter 19, of the *History of the English Church and its People*.

[4] Bede's acrostic poem, honoring many virgin saints in celebration of Æthelthryth's virtue, appears in book IV, chapter 20.

[5] Elizabeth Stevens and Pauline Thompson, eds., "Gregory of Ely's Verse Life and Miracles of St Æthelthryth," *Analecta Bollandiana* 106.3–4 (1988): 333–90.

prose version of her life was also written around the same time. Her legend also appears in a later Anglo-Norman text.[6]

In addition to Bede's veneration of her story, evidence for the popularity of this saint's cult is widespread in England before 1100. Her feast day is recorded in the tenth-century *Benedictional of Æthelwold* and in six early martyrologies,[7] including the late ninth-century *Old English Martyrology*, as well as twenty-two religious calendars.[8] Æthelthryth also appears in twenty-six Anglo-Saxon litanies dated before 1100 and in twelve dedications from early churches built before 1700. Interest in her legend was especially evident after Æthelwold re-established Ely as a monastery exclusively for male monks in c.963. In addition to the manuscript used for this translation, three other manuscripts from Anglo-Saxon England preserve portions of her life. As the text translated here makes clear, Ælfric derives his version of Æthelthryth's life from Bede's Anglo-Latin text. Æthelthryth is Ælfric's only native English female saint as well as his only non-martyred female saint.

Life of Saint Æthelthryth

Although it may be miraculous, now we will write about that holy Saint Æthelthryth, the English maiden who had two husbands, but even so remained a maiden, as the miracles which she often works reveal.

Her father was king of the East Angles. He was called Anna and was a very Christian man as he proved with deeds. All his family became celebrated through God.[9] When Æthelthryth was given to a certain nobleman as a wife,[10] the Almighty God did not want her maidenhood to be destroyed with fornication, so He preserved her

---

6   See Jocelyn Wogan-Browne, "Rerouting the Dower: The Anglo-Norman Life of St Audrey by Marie (of Chatteris?)" in *Power of the Weak: Studies on Medieval Women*, ed. Jennifer Carpenter and Sally-Beth MacLean (Toronto: University of Toronto, 1995), pp. 27–56.

7   In addition to the OEM, mention of Æthelthryth appears in martyrologies by Ado, Bede, Florus, Hrabanus, Lyons, and Usuard.

8   St Willibrord, MCR, and twenty in Wormald.

9   Anna's four daughters (Æthelthryth, Sexburg, Æthelburg, and Wihtburg) were all well known religious figures in the seventh century. Æthelthryth, Sexburg, and Wihtburg were all buried at the monastery at Ely.

10 Æthelthryth married her first husband, Tondberht, in c.652.

purity, because He is God Almighty and can do anything He wishes. He reveals His power in many ways. The nobleman died when God wanted it, and she was given to King Ecgfrid.[11] For twelve years, the maiden lived unstained in her marriage to this king. As the miracles of her glory and her maidenhood make evident, she loved the Savior, who preserved her chastity and honored the servants of God.

One of the servants whom she especially loved was the Bishop Wilfrid.[12] He told Bede that King Ecgfrid would often promise him much land and money, if he could persuade Æthelthryth, his wife, to enjoy his marriage. Now the holy Bede, who composed this book, said that the Almighty God could easily make it possible for Æthelthryth to remain an unstained maiden, even though she had a husband, in our own day, as it was in ancient days, by means of the same God who dwells always with His chosen saints as He Himself has promised.

Æthelthryth wanted to abandon all worldly things and earnestly begged the king that she be allowed to serve Christ in the monastic way of life as her heart inspired her. Although it was a long while until she had what she desired, when the king gave her leave, Bishop Wilfrid consecrated[13] her to a convent.[14] Then, she lived in that monastery for about twelve months. After this, she became consecrated as an abbess over many nuns at the monastery of Ely. By her good example, she preserved them as if she were their mother in the spiritual life.

It is written about her that she led her life well by fasting, except for one meal, unless it was a feast day, and that she greatly loved solitary prayer. She wore woolen clothes and would rarely bathe her body, except on high holy days, when she would bathe first all those who were in the monastery, minister to them with her maid-servant, and then bathe herself.

---

[11] Since her father had died in c.654, Æthelthryth's second marriage was arranged by her uncle Æthelwold, who succeeded Anna as king of East Anglia. Æthelthryth married Ecgfrid, the son and heir to Oswy of Northumbria in c.660. Ecgfrid was said to have been fourteen years old when he married Æthelthryth.

[12] Wilfrid was a powerful bishop of Northumbria. He traveled to Rome to acquire permission from Pope Benedict II for Æthelthryth to found the monastery at Ely.

[13] The Old English term here is *gehadode*, which literally means *hooded*. It refers to a ceremony in which women were consecrated as nuns to monastic orders. In this ceremony, a bishop or priest would "hood" them with a veil, indicating their spiritual marriage to Christ.

[14] The first convent in which Æthelthryth lived was at Coldingham, near Berwickshire. Æthelthryth's aunt Ebba was the abbess of this monastery during the time Æthelthryth lived there.

In the eighth year after she was made abbess, she grew ill, as she had earlier predicted, until one tumor grew on her neck, large under her chin bone.[15] After this, she greatly thanked God that she suffered such a hardship on her neck.

She said, "Because I adorned my neck in youth with numerous necklaces, I know I absolutely deserve that my neck should be afflicted with such an illness. It seems to me that the grace of God might cleanse my guilt, since this tumor shines on me now, instead of gold, and this burning heat, instead of lofty gems."

There was a certain physician called Cynefryth in the company of the faithful, and some of them said that this physician should lance the tumor. When he did so, at once corrupt matter[16] fell out of it. Afterward, it seemed to them that she might recover, but she departed from the world with glory to God on the third day after the wound was opened. She was buried, as she herself had requested, among her sisters in a wooden casket.

After her death, her sister Sexburg,[17] who earlier had been a queen in Canterbury, was consecrated as abbess. Sixteen years later, Sexburg wanted the bones of her sister to be brought up from her tomb, and carried into the church. She sent the brothers[18] to seek a special stone for such a purpose, because there are few hewn stones in the marsh.

They rowed then to Grantchester,[19] so hastened by God that they immediately discovered a single great coffin wrought from marble stone standing there against the wall above the earth. It was all white in color, and its lid, also of white marble stone, fitted so perfectly it was as though God had formed it.

Thanking God, the brothers joyfully took the coffin and brought it

---

[15] The description of her illness suggests that Æthelthryth most likely contracted bubonic plague.

[16] The Old English term, *wyrms*, is also cognate with the word *worms*, but the alternative meaning of some sort of poisonous fluid seems more accurate here.

[17] Sexburg is Æthelthryth's sister in the literal sense. Another of Anna's daughters, Sexburg also achieved much recognition for her religious activities. In *Forgetful of their Sex:Female Sanctity and Society, ca 500–1100* (Chicago: University of Chicago Press, 1998), Jane Tibbetts Schulenburg notes that in the Anglo-Saxon period "the office of abbess was frequently kept within the family and passed from one sister to another," p. 278.

[18] Both men and women lived in the double monastery of Ely, founded by Æthelthryth.

[19] Located near Cambridge, Grantchester was originally a Roman settlement, suggesting that the marble coffin, which the monks discover there, was probably of Roman origin.

to the monastery. Since she wanted the bones gathered, the abbess Sexburg commanded that a tent be raised above the tomb. Then, they all sang psalms and elegies while someone opened the tomb from above. She lay there in the casket as if she was asleep, whole in all her limbs. The physician who had opened the tumor was there, and he carefully examined her. The wound on which the physician had previously worked was healed, and those same garments in which she had been wound were as intact as if they had been completely new.

Sexburg greatly rejoiced for her sister. After they had washed the soulless body and reverently wound her with new garments, they bore her into the church.[20] Then, exalting her with songs, they laid her in the coffin, where she lies in great reverence until this day, as a miracle to people.

It was also miraculous that the coffin was wrought through God's foresight, so that it fit her as if she herself had constructed it. The stone at her head was hewn so that it was precisely measured to the holy maiden's head. Because her body would not decay in the earth, it is clear that she was an unstained maiden. Through her, God's power is truly made manifest, since He can exalt decayed bodies, He who has preserved her body whole in the coffin even until this day. May it be to Him an eternal glory.

As we heard long ago, many sick people have been healed there through this holy woman, and also those who touched any part of the garment with which she was wound were immediately healed. The casket in which she first was laid benefitted many people, as the teacher Bede said in the book he wrote. Also, as the book tells us, laymen often have preserved their purity in marriage for the love of Christ, as we could relate if you would care to hear it. We will tell, however, about one particular noble who lived with his wife in chastity for thirty years. Except for the three sons he had, for thirty years they lived without fornication. Until the husband entered a monastic way of life, they also worked many alms. As the books tell us, at his death, the angels of the Lord came at once and, with songs, carried his soul to Heaven. There are many such examples in the books, concerning how often husbands and wives have behaved so wondrously and lived in chastity for the glory of the Savior who established purity in them. To Christ our Savior there is always honor and glory in eternity. AMEN.

[20] The translation of Æthelthryth's miraculously preserved body into its new tomb is recorded as occurring on October 17. This date appears in some religious calendars in addition to Æthelthryth's June 23 feast day.

Agatha

Extremely popular from early in Christian history through the Middle Ages, Saint Agatha's biography inspired the actions and stories of several other Christian martyrs, including Saint Lucy, whose legend is also translated in this collection. While no reliable records survive to document this saint's history, tradition supports the later Latin life's assertion that Agatha was martyred in c.250–53, during the persecution of the Roman emperor Decian. Although her legend names Catania as the location for her martyrdom, the cities of both Palermo and Catania in Sicily claim to be her birthplace. This virgin martyr is honored on the feast day of February 5.

The earliest evidence for public veneration of Agatha appears in documents from the end of the fifth century. A letter from Gelasius, pope in c.492–96, mentions a church of St Agatha. Several Latin poems from the sixth century also celebrate Agatha.[1] The earliest Latin version[2] of the complete legend of Agatha was composed in the sixth century. A Greek text[3] of Agatha's life, probably based on the Latin version, also exists from the sixth century. In medieval Europe, the legend of Agatha was one of the most popular women saints' lives. Her name is mentioned in several early religious calendars and martyrologies from Western Europe.[4] At least forty texts containing versions of one recension of Agatha's Latin life survive in continental manuscripts dated before 1100.

Agatha's cult was known in Anglo-Saxon England no later than the late seventh or early eighth centuries. Most notably from this time, Agatha is mentioned in Bede's martyrology, in a poem by Bede in praise of virginity,[5] and in Aldhelm's *Carmen de Virginitate*. Although her story is not recounted in the ninth-century *Old English Martyrology*, Agatha's name is included in fifty pre-1100 Anglo-Saxon litanies, and in dedications to four early English churches

---

[1] See, for example, Venantius Fortunatus's *De Virginitate* (Carmen 8:4). A hymn originally thought to be by Damasus, a pope c.366–84, but actually from somewhat later also survives: *Hymn to St Agatha*, PL 13:403.

[2] AS Feb. 1, p. 595; BHL 133–36.

[3] BHG 36–37.

[4] Among these are the martyrologies of Florus and Hieronymian.

[5] Bede's *History*, book IV, chapter 20.

dated prior to 1700. A tenth-century metrical calendar (MCR) from Anglo-Saxon England also mentions Agatha. From the tenth century on, portions of the *Life of St Agatha*, along with the *Life of St Agnes* also translated in this collection, were used in England for liturgical purposes, specifically in those liturgies in which nuns were consecrated to their order and made their permanent vows of virginity.[6] In addition to the manuscript used for this translation, portions of Agatha's life appear in two other Anglo-Saxon manuscripts dated before 1100. Anglo-Norman versions of Agatha's legend also survive in manuscripts from the twelfth and thirteenth centuries.

Life of Saint Agatha

There was one particular fortunate maiden called Agatha, wise and devout, in the city of Sicily at the time when the cruel and blood-thirsty persecutor Quintianus ruled the province under the emperor. Subject to his own lustfulness, he was greedy and miserly, a slave of the Devil, and he despised the Lord.

When he heard about Agatha's demeanor, he pondered how he could get that maiden for himself. He commanded that she be delivered to a certain debased woman called Aphrodisia, who was shameful in her habits. She had nine daughters, who were also lascivious and disgraceful. For thirty nights, he wanted Agatha to learn their practices so that her mind would be perverted by the seductions of these prostitutes. So, with her nine daughters, that disgraceful woman Aphrodisia tormented Agatha. Sometimes she would act alluringly, sometimes terrifyingly, in order to pervert Agatha's mind.

"Your words are like wind, but they cannot uproot my steadfast thought which is firmly grounded," Agatha said to the evil brood.

Weeping, she said that she wanted to endure deadly torture for Christ's name, "even as a thirsty person longs for a wellspring or cooling waters in the heat of the sun."[7]

When Aphrodisia saw she could not bend the mind of the maiden with her shameful temptations, she went to Quintianus and said to him, "Stones may soften and stiff iron become like molten lead, before the faith in Agatha's breast can be ever extinguished. Day and

---

6   M. Teresa Tavormina discusses this at some length in "Of Maidenhood and Maternity: Liturgical Hagiography and the Medieval Ideal of Virginity," *American Benedictine Review* 31.4 (December 1980): 384–99.

7   Proverbs 25:25.

night, I and my daughters could not accomplish anything. Even though we constantly enticed her to consent to you, it profited us little. I offered her gems, clothes of gold, and other favors, as well as a huge home and servants, but she rejected all that as if it were the dung which lies under foot."[8]

Quintianus became enraged and commanded that she be fetched quickly. First, he asked her about her birth.[9]

"I come from nobility, as all my family would witness," Agatha said.

Then, the judge asked, "Why do you conduct yourself by means of lowly habits, as though you were a female slave?"

"I am God's handmaid," Agatha answered, "and anyone who wants to be a servant of Christ is greatly ennobled."

"What then, do we not have any nobility because we reject servitude to your Christ?" Quintianus asked the maiden of Christ.

Agatha answered the wicked man by saying, "Your nobility is a disgraceful imprisonment, because you would be a servant to sin and stones."

Quintianus, the murderous torturer, replied, "We can easily punish you, no matter what you insult with your raving mouth! Even so, before you come to the aforesaid tortures, explain why you scorn the practices of our gods."

"You've said nothing about any gods, but about cruel devils. You change their likenesses into ore and stone and, overlay all the sculptures with art," thus Agatha answered the wicked man.

Then, Quintianus said that she must choose whether she would die among the condemned for her folly or whether she would sacrifice to the gods, as though nobly-born and wise.

Steadily, Agatha said to him, "May your wife be one such as your foul goddess Venus, and may you be as your scandalous god Jove, so that you two also may be counted among the gods."

At this, Quintianus commanded that she be struck repeatedly on the cheek, until she could not utter a sound.

Afterward, Agatha again said the same words.

---

8 This concept of the woman saint rejecting worldly possessions as if they were dung also appears in the *Life of St Agnes* and the *Life of St Eugenia*.

9 Although it follows the Latin source fairly closely, the dialogue between Agatha and Quintianus that follows has been condensed and adapted in such a way that it resembles the structure of the Germanic literary convention known as a *flyting*, a highly patterned verbal exchange between two antagonists that includes insults and incitements to action.

"You have made it clear that you prefer to suffer tortures. Now you repeat insults to me!" Quintianus said.

That maiden answered, "I am greatly astonished that you, an intelligent person, have bowed to great folly. Those you have as gods you would be ashamed to imitate. Even if they were true gods, I wish you would adopt God. If you would shun them, then we two might speak as one. I promise they are so evil and so unclean that you would curse a person if you wished that his life be like that of your loathsome gods."

"Why do you cry out so many vain words? Sacrifice to the gods, so that I will not cruelly destroy you," Quintianus said.

Unafraid, Agatha answered the judge, "If you hunt me now with wild beasts, they will be hand-tamed at once by the name of the Savior. If you prepare a fire for me, there will come a wholesome dew suddenly out of heaven from the angels of the Lord. If you threaten me with whips, I will have the Holy Ghost through whom I will scorn all your whips."

The judge shook his diabolical head and commanded her be taken to a solitary windowless prison. He commanded that she should think about how she might escape from the murderous tortures.

"Poor wretch, you yourself should consider how you might escape from eternal punishments!" Agatha said.

In bliss, she entered the windowless prison, as though she were invited to a luscious banquet,[10] entrusting her struggle to the benevolent Lord.

In the morning, the sinful judge commanded that Agatha be brought into his loathsome presence. He asked what she had concluded about her safety.

"Christ is salvation for me," Agatha said.

The judge asked, "How long will you foolishly prolong this by praising Christ? Forsake your Christ and invoke the gods, unless you want to lose your young life!"

"Forsake your gods, who are stone and wood. Pray to your Creator who truly lives. If you renounce Him, you shall suffer eternal punishments," Agatha answered succinctly.

Furious, the wicked man commanded that she be stretched on the rack and cruelly twisted like a rope. "Abandon your stubbornness, so that your life might be saved," he said.

---

[10] The convention of the saint's attitude toward torture or death as pleasurable is also found in the *Life of St Cecilia,* which describes Valerian and Tiburtius welcoming their death in language similar to this passage.

"I am as desirous for these loathsome tortures as he who sees what he desires, or he who discovers many gold-hoards," Agatha answered from the rack. "My soul cannot be taken into Heaven in joy, unless my body be confined in your bonds and gripped in the fetters of your executioners."

The cruel one became enraged. He commanded that her breasts be twisted on the rack and then he commanded that one be cut off.

"Oh you most disgraceful one! Does it not shame you to cut off that which you yourself wanted to suck? But I have my breast sound in my soul, because I am completely fed by my senses," Agatha said to him.

At this, Quintianus ordered her to be led into the prison. He commanded that food and water be withheld from her and that no physician be allowed to treat her.

Even so, a certain gray-haired man, with his servant before him, came into the prison in the middle of the night. He had a torch in his hands and wanted to treat the saint.

The blessed Agatha said to the physician, "I have never been treated by any leechcraft in my life. I have my Savior who heals with His word. If He wishes, He can heal me mightily."

"He sent me to you. I am His apostle[11] and, in His name, even now you are made whole," the gray-haired man said and then he left at once.

Agatha kneeled and thanked Christ that He had remembered to send His famous apostle to her with such comfort. After praying, she looked at her breast which had been cut off and, through Christ, it had been restored and all her wounds were healed. Then, a great light shone in that dark prison, until the guards fled, seized by fear. At this, the prisoners urged the holy maiden to get away and escape the tortures.

But, that noble maiden Agatha said, "I will not delay my royal crown,[12] nor trouble the guards. I will remain here."

On the fifth day, the judge commanded that she be fetched and said that she should sacrifice to the gods or be tormented with severe tortures.

"You poor, senseless man, who invokes stone and not the true God, who healed me in His name from all the punishments which you violently attached to my body! He restored my breast which you cruelly cut off," Agatha said.

[11] Tradition identifies the apostle as St Peter.
[12] II Timothy 4:8.

When the idolater asked who had healed her, Agatha said, "Christ, God's son."

"Still you name Christ!" Quintianus said to the pure maiden.

"I acknowledge Christ with my lips and will always call him with my heart," she answered.

Then, the Devil's vassal said, " Now I will see if Christ heals you!"

He commanded that many burning embers and shattered tiles be strewn over the floor and that she be rolled naked in the fire. At this, there was a great earthquake in that same place and a stone wall fell upon the advisor of the stupid one, until he was completely crushed, together with some other retainer, very rightly so because they had been advisors of the cruel judge for his evil deeds.

Moreover, the city kept shaking because of the earthquake. The city-dwellers all ran together to the cruel one, asking in a loud tumult why he had tormented the maiden of God so harshly.

Extremely frightened because of the tumult and also because of the earthquake, Quintianus fled then. Nevertheless, he ordered her to be taken into the prison.

Thus, with outstretched hands, Agatha inwardly called out to the Savior, "Oh You, my Lord, who created me as a human and from childhood until this have shielded me always! You who have turned worldly love away from me! You who have made it possible for me to overcome the tortures of sharp iron and fire, and the rending hooks of the executioners! You who have granted me patience in the tortures! Now I beg You, Lord, that You take my spirit to You, because it is time now that I abandon this world, and come to Your gracious mercy, my beloved Lord."

After praying this inside the prison, she gave up her spirit and journeyed to God. Afterward, a city-dweller buried her body in a completely new tomb with much reverence.

Later, there came an angel of God, walking like a man, with many beautiful youths following at his feet. Inside the tomb at the maiden's head, he placed a marble stone inscribed with these words, "Mentem sanctum spontaneam, honorem deo, et patrie liberationem" (which in English is, "A voluntarily holy heart, an honor to the benevolent God, and a redemption for the country").[13]

The angel then turned away with the youths and no one in the district had seen them before.

So, the enemy of Christ Quintianus journeyed in a ship over

---

[13] Leviticus 25:24.

Semithetus,[14] regarding Agatha's possessions. He also wanted to arrest all her kinsmen, but he was not able because of Christ. A horse seized him with its teeth as he lay on the ship. When another horse kicked out, it violently heaved him up and flung him overboard. His foul body was never found afterward. Frightened by God, no one dared torment her kinsmen after this, but instead they revered them all.

In the same region of the land of Sicily is a burning mountain, heated with sulphur (which in English is brimstone), which people call Etna. The mountain always burns more intensely than others. About twelve months after Agatha's suffering, Etna happened to blow up. With a fearsome conflagration, it flowed around the mountain as if it were a flood, and it melted the stones. The earth burned, until it came to the city.

Then, the heathens ran to the holy tomb, and from the holy tomb, lifted the veil before the fire, which frightened them severely. At this, the fire was extinguished and immediately stood still, because of the efforts of Agatha, that noble young woman. It burned for six days and stood still on the day the blessed Agatha had departed to the eternal life, so that it would be evident that the city was saved from the fire's harm through Agatha's intercession. As praise to the Savior, who so honors His saints, let this be always a glory to Him in the eternal world. AMEN.

---

[14] Skeat identifies this as the river Symaethus.

Agnes

As with most of the early women saints, reliable historical documentation for the existence of a Christian martyr named Agnes is almost non-existent. All we know with any certainty is that a Christian martyr by this name was buried in a cemetery on the Via Nomentana in Rome late in the third or very early in the fourth century. Yet, almost immediately after this Christian was martyred, the story of a twelve-year-old virgin martyr of the same name began circulating widely in Christian circles. While it proves nothing definitive about the life of an actual Agnes on whom this legend may have been based, such an immediate interest in the story of this virgin martyr suggests it may have had historical origins. From the beginning, her feast day has been celebrated on January 21. The fact that no early records provide alternative feast days for this saint also may lend credibility to early certainty concerning the legend of Agnes.

From the mid-fourth century on, Saint Agnes was held in high esteem by the early Christian church. The story of Constantia, daughter of the emperor Constantine (c.274–337), appended to the life of Agnes and translated here, supports veneration of her cult in the fourth century with its mention of the church Constantia built in Agnes' honor. Early mention of her legend appears in a sermon by St Ambrose in c.377[1] and in an inscription on a monument to her commissioned by St Damasus, who was pope in c.366–84. Also by the late fourth century, Augustine[2] and Prudentius[3] had also praised her heroic efforts to preserve her virginity and faith. Her name also appears in religious calendars from this time.[4] The life of Agnes first appears in a late fourth- or early fifth-century Greek version, on which the fifth-century Latin text[5] of the saint's life is based. In Western Europe, throughout the medieval period, the legend of

---

[1] *De Virginibus* 1:2 (in PL 16:200–02).

[2] *Sermo* 273:6 (in PL 38:1251).

[3] *Peristephanon*, Hymn 14:10 (in Ruinart's *Acta Sincera Martyrum*, ed. Ratisbon, 1859).

[4] See, for example, the *Depositio Martyrum* (in Ruinart's *Acta Sincera Martyrum*, ed. Ratisbon, 1859).

[5] AS Jan. 2:350–63; BHL 156–57.

Agnes occurs in at least forty-three manuscripts dated before 1100 and in many of the most influential early martyrologies and calendars.[6]

Evidence for the cult of Agnes in Anglo-Saxon England is widespread beginning as early as the late seventh or early eighth centuries. During this time, both Aldhelm and Bede honor her in poems praising Christian virgins.[7] Both the martyrology composed by Bede and the anonymous ninth-century *Old English Martyrology* record her feast day. Her name appears in forty-three litanies and twenty-two calendars[8] from Anglo-Saxon England, as well as in five dedications in early English churches built before 1700. In addition to the base manuscript used for this translation, some portion of the *Life of St Agnes* is included in three Anglo-Saxon manuscripts dated before 1100. Along with the *Life of St Agatha*, material from the *Life of St Agnes* was included in English liturgical ceremonies after the tenth century, in which nuns made their permanent vows to their religious orders and to a life of virginity.[9] Anglo-Norman versions of her life also appear in manuscripts from the twelfth and thirteenth centuries.

Life of Saint Agnes

Ambrose, bishop from Milan, learned about the blessed Agnes in ancient books; how she endured cruel persecution in the city of Rome and suffered martyrdom in maidenhood. This is what Ambrose wrote[10] about the maiden.

In the city of Rome at that time, there was a certain maiden of noble birth called Agnes, who believed in the Savior. She was innocent and wise, young in years, but old in spirit. Through faith, she struggled against fiendish lords, and when she was thirteen she surrendered to death and achieved eternal life because she loved Christ. She was beautiful in form and more beautiful in faith.

Once when she returned from school, a particular retainer, the son of Simpronius, who was prefect over the city and an idolater, wooed her. Afterward, his relatives immediately offered the maiden costly

---

[6] These include Ado, Florus, Hieronymian, and Lyons.

[7] See Aldhelm's *Carmen de Virginitate* and Bede's *History*, book IV, chapter 20.

[8] Among these are Bede's martyrology, MCR, OEM, Willibrord, and twenty calendars in Wormald.

[9] M. Teresa Tavormina discusses such liturgical ceremonies in "Of Maidenhood and Maternity: Liturgical Hagiography and the Medieval Ideal of Virginity," *American Benedictine Review* 31.4 (December 1980): 384–99.

[10] See St Ambrose, *De Virginibus* I:2.

garments, and promised her even more precious ones, but the blessed Agnes rejected all that, caring no more about those treasures than about the reek of dung.[11]

The retainer brought the pure maiden precious gems and worldly adornments, and promised her riches if she would desire him.

"Leave me, you burning sin, fuel of vices, and food of death! Depart from me!" Agnes strongly answered the retainer. "I have another lover more noble than you, who has promised me better adornments.[12] He has given me His ring of faith as His pledge, and He has bestowed me with inconceivable honors. He has encircled my right hand, as well as my neck, with precious stones and shining gems. He has put His mark upon my face, so that I would love no other over Him. He has dressed me with a robe woven of gold, and has adorned me with bountiful necklaces. Further, He has shown me His splendid hoards, which He has promised to me, if I would follow Him. I cannot insult Him by choosing another, and I will not abandon Him, who has betrothed me with love."

"His appearance is more beautiful and His love more delightful. His bridal bed is now already prepared for me with delights. His maidens sing to me with harmonious voices. From His mouth, I receive milk and honey. Even now, His pure arms embrace me. His fair body is united with mine, and His blood decorates my eyebrows.[13] His mother is a virgin, and His mighty father did not enjoy a wife. Angels always bow to Him. The delightful stars, sun and moon, which light the world, glorify His beauty. Through His speech, the dead are revived and, through His touch, the weakened ill are strengthened. His powers do not fail, nor do His riches fade."

"With all devotion, I will always keep my promise to the one to whom I have committed myself. When I love Him, I am completely pure. When I touch Him, I am unstained. When I submit to Him, I am still a maiden. Yet, children will not fail in this marriage, where there is conception without pain, and continual fertility."

The retainer grew angry, and was blinded within, after the speech of this maiden who had spurned him with words. He grew ill and, sighing deeply from inside his breast, he lay in bed. Physicians tried

---

[11] This concept of the woman saint rejecting worldly possessions as if they were dung also appears in the *Life of St Agatha* and in the *Life of St Eugenia*.

[12] In the speech that follows, Agnes uses imagery evocative of the Song of Songs.

[13] Literally, the Old English term here means *eye-rings*, possibly suggesting that cosmetic enhancement of the eyes was fashionable, as eye-shadow make-up is fashionable today.

to discover why he was lying down, and reported the mental state of the retainer to his father.

At once the father sent that same message to the maiden, which his son had asked earlier. But, Agnes refused, saying she would never defile the noble trust of her first bridegroom with any other betrothal.

In the mind of the prefect, it seemed outrageous that she would consider another over his child. Even so, proudly, he inquired rigorously who the bridegroom was that Agnes praised. He was told that she had been a Christian from childhood, and that she was so filled with sorcery that she considered Christ her bridegroom.

So, Simpronius loudly commanded that she be brought from home to his judgment seat. First, he charmed the maiden privately with sweet words, and after that he threatened her. But, no flattery could seduce God's maiden away from her beloved Lord, and she was not afraid of his threats.

When Simpronius saw her determination was genuine, he made it clear to her friends that she would be condemned because of her Christianity, which the emperor detested. In the morning, the evil judge again commanded that the blessed Agnes be brought to him, and he told her many times how his son loved her. But, even though he spoke much, he succeeded little.

Sorrowfully, he sat on his judgment seat, and promised the maiden numerous punishments, unless she would reject the true Savior. Then, again he said to the wise maiden, "Listen to my advice. Quickly, if you love maidenhood, submit to the practices of the goddess Vesta, who shuns wantonness."

"I rejected your son, who is a true man. I cannot look on his face, because of my love for Christ. How can I cause Him injury by humbling myself to dead idols?" Agnes answered the cruel one.

"I have tolerated you until this," the prefect said to the holy maiden, "because you are still a child, but you insult our gods, even though you have not yet angered them."

Agnes replied, "The Almighty is more aware of the minds of men than of their age. Faith is not measured in years, but in keen understanding. Let your gods be enraged, if they can be anything. Let them summon us themselves, so that we would pray to them. If you can do this, you can afflict us however you want."

At this, the shameful judge Simpronius said, "Choose now, Agnes, whether you will offer your sacrifice with the maidens of the great Vesta, or whether you will have to cooperate with loathsome prostitutes, and be foully disgraced. The Christians will not be able to save you then!"

With great resolve, Agnes responded, "If you knew my God, you would not say these words. I reject your threats completely and without concern, because I know the power of my Lord. Because He is a wall of strength to me, an indefatigable protection, I trust in Him, so that I need not sacrifice to your accursed gods, nor will I ever be degraded by the pollution of strangers as a debased prostitute. I have a holy angel of God with me. Your gods are melted from ore, from which a person builds pleasing vessels, or they are stone, with which a person builds streets. There is no dwelling of God in the gray stones, nor in the brass wedges; instead, He dwells in Heaven. Truly, the terrible, greedy fire of Hell will seize you and those like you! You will not be consumed, but always you will be regenerated by the eternal flames."

The insane judge commanded that her clothes be removed and that she be led naked to the house of the fornicator. To make this known, he ordered that it be called out through the streets.

The power of God then became very evident for, as soon as the executioners destroyed her clothes, the maiden's hair completely enveloped her.[14] Equally on every side, her hair covered her. When they dragged the maiden to the prostitute's house, she met an angel of God there, shining so brilliantly that no one could see or touch her. Because of the great light, shining over the whole house as bright as the sun in the day, the more intently they gazed at her, the more their eyes were dazzled.

Praying to the Almighty, Agnes prostrated herself, and God sent her a shining tunic. She thanked Christ then and put on the clothes. So that people could see that God had sent her the tunic, it shone brilliantly and was measured exactly to fit her.

Afterward, the house of the prostitutes became a chapel for people. Each of those who went inside worshiped God, because of the heavenly light which shone on the house.

When the son of the prefect arrived with his shameful companions at the shining shrine, he wanted to defile God's handmaid. He sent some of them ahead, but they marveled greatly at the beautiful light and returned amazed to their disgraceful lord.

Because they had marveled so at the shining light and would not dare stain her, he threatened them severely. Then, with a shameful

---

[14] The presence of long hair on a woman is normally associated with sexuality and licentiousness in late antiquity and the Middle Ages, but here the common convention is reversed and Agnes' hair becomes the salvation of her body, rather than an advertisement of its sinfulness.

desire, he himself ran inside. But, he fell outstretched in front of the maiden, killed by the Devil, whom he foolishly obeyed. He lay there dead on the floor for a long time. Since his companions assumed he was occupied with his disgraceful deeds, one of them went to visit. As soon as he found him dead, he cried out sadly, "Oh you ever glorious Romans, help us quickly! This cruel prostitute has destroyed our lord with her sorcery!"

Then, a frightened city-dweller ran away from there, and immediately the father arrived, calling out with a loud cry, "You fiercest woman! Would you reveal your fiendish sorcery by killing my son?"

Agnes said to him, "Why are the others who went inside here alive? They worship the Almighty God, who mercifully clothed me. He sent me His angel, who preserved my body, which was consecrated to Christ from the cradle. Your shameless son, with shameful intentions, ran to me, but the angel killed him, and delivered him to the Devil who destroyed him right away."

"Your story will be made clear, if now you will pray to the same angel to raise up sound my only son," the prefect said to the holy maiden.

"You are not worthy to see that miracle," the blessed Agnes answered. "Even so, it is time the might of the Lord should be made evident. Now all of you go outside, so that I can pray alone by myself."

Once they had all gone outside, she prayed alone by herself, begging her Lord to raise up the dead man. At this, an angel of Christ appeared and raised the retainer. After he had been revived, right away he ran outside, calling this out all over, "There is one God in Heaven and also on earth, He who is the God of the Christians, and your gods are nothing! They cannot benefit themselves nor others."

At this, the idol-worshipers became extremely upset, shouting about the faithful maiden, "Take her away! Quickly take away the cruel witch, who has turned the minds of the people with her witchcraft!"

Since the prefect dared not do anything against the idol-worshipers, he left his servants to the quarreling. Sorrowfully, he traveled away by himself, because after his son had arisen, he could not save that maiden from the idolaters.

When the proconsul Aspasius could not oppose the murderous people, he commanded that a huge fire be kindled that would cause much damage, and that she be thrown into the middle of it. It was done as the bloodthirsty one commanded, but immediately the flame divided itself in two, and burned up those who had instigated the quarreling.

In its midst, the blessed Agnes stood completely safe.

With outstretched hands, she prayed, "Oh You Almighty God, I pray only to the terrible Creator, who is worshiped truly as the father of my Lord, whom I bless, because I escaped those cruel threats and also the filth of the Devil. Because of Your delightful Son, I am evenly covered with sacred dew, this flame is divided, and the unbelievers burned up. I bless You, famous Father God, that unafraid I could travel through the fire to You. Because I have seen it, I believe it. That which I have hoped for, I now have. With my mouth, my heart, and everything within, I praise You! I desire only You, the true God, who rules always with Your Son and the Holy Ghost, the one Almighty God."

That fire was so quenched that not one coal glowed there. The people attributed it to sorcery. Roaring, they were angry for her life. Since Aspasius could not stand the great uproar, he commanded that she be killed with a deadly sword. Then, Christ received her, martyred in His name.

In great bliss, her father and mother took her body. Without grief, they brought her to their property, and buried her there.[15] They watched there frequently, honoring that shrine.

One night, a great maidenly company came to them with Agnes in their midst. They were all arrayed in golden apparel, and traveled gloriously within a tremendous light.

"Take heed that you do not weep for me as dead, but rejoice with me!" Saint Agnes said to her family. "I am united with these maidens, receive fair dwellings with them, and am joined to Him in Heaven, whom I loved here on earth."

After these words, she departed with the maidens, and this vision became widely celebrated.

A little while later, in the days of the emperor who was called Constantine, some people happened to tell his daughter, Constantia, about the vision. Even though she was still a heathen, she was wise. She was extremely ill and had dreadful wounds on all her limbs.

One night, she decided she would watch at Agnes' tomb to pray for her healing. Although she was a heathen, she came there with a faithful heart, and called to the maiden, who owned the tomb, that she would grant her healing.

She fell asleep, and in a dream saw the blessed Agnes, saying these words to her, "You, noble Constantia, resolutely begin to

---

[15] The sepulchre in which Agnes was buried was located on the Via Nomentana in Rome.

believe that the Savior can heal you. Through Him, you shall receive the healing of your wounds."

When Constantia awoke, she was healed so that no painful wounds were visible on her body. Whole, she traveled home to her father. With him and her brothers, she rejoiced. All the servants rejoiced for her health. Heathenism waned and belief in God waxed. Afterward, she was baptized, as was her father, and received the veil of the fair way of life. Through her illustrious example, many other maidens renounced worldly pleasures and were consecrated to Christ.

Constantia asked her father Constantine to raise up a church for the blessed Agnes and commanded that a coffin be placed there for herself. Fame of this spread through all the region, and many ill people came to the holy tomb and were healed by Saint Agnes. Afterward, many Roman maidens remained pure in maidenhood also for the love of Christ, according to the example of Agnes, who is buried there.

Another story written by Terentianus[16]

In those days, there was a certain general called Gallicanus, who was victorious in battle. Because of his great victories, the emperor loved him fully, even though he was not baptized. When the Scythians were fighting greatly against him, he wooed Constantia, daughter of the emperor.

The emperor grew concerned about the wooing, because he knew his daughter, who had chosen the Lord, would rather perish than marry.

When his daughter saw her father's distress, with pure intention, she said to him, "I know that God will never abandon me. Cast aside your worry and promise the general that he will receive me after the battle, once he has overcome the Scythians with victory. Because of this promise, I will take his daughters, Attica and Arthemia, for my companions, until our dowries have been arranged. Let John and Paul, those most trusted by me, travel with him to the army. They shall tell him my habits, and I shall discover his habits through his daughters."

So, it was done that she received the daughters and the general went to the army. At once, Constantia prayed with great fervor to God that he would hear her request, "Oh You Almighty God, who,

---

[16] Here the Old English manuscript appends the story of Constantia to Agnes's legend and attributes it to the Roman writer Terentianus.

because of the intercession of Your illustrious martyr Agnes, have healed my leprosy and have revealed Your true love for me, as you promised us in Your Holy Gospel. I tell You truly that my father will give You whatever You ask him in my name. I beg You, Lord, that You take for Yourself these maidens and their father Gallicanus, who wants to marry me in order to take my purity away from Your faith. Open their hearts' ears to the teaching of redemption, so that they will love only You, and will not desire earthly things, and will come to Your bridal bed burning with love."

After this prayer, the maidens submitted to the holy baptism, and were consecrated in purity to the Savior before their father arrived. Then, Gallicanus also converted to God, and prayed to him with true belief at the shrine of St Peter, which stands within Rome.

With joy, the emperor welcomed him, saying, "When you went into battle, you sacrificed to the foul devils. Now that you have returned victorious, you yourself pray to Christ and to his apostles. Explain how this might be."

Gallicanus bowed to the faithful emperor and told the order of how he had been converted to God, "The Scythian people had slain many of ours, and I was trapped in one little city with a small force. We did not dare fight against the huge army that had surrounded the city. After this, I frequently offered my sacrifices to the gods, until my comrades delivered me and themselves to the attacking enemies. Then, I took flight. The Christians, John and Paul, said, 'Promise Heavenly God that you will convert to Him, if He helps you now, and you will have victory.' "

"Since those saints persuaded me, I promised and immediately an angel of God with a cross came to me. He commanded me to take up my sword and go with him. I followed him, and many angels came in the semblance of gloriously armed men. With their words, they encouraged me and commanded me to go forth until we came to the king. When he fell afraid, outstretched at my feet, those champions of God bound King Bard and his two sons, entrusting them to me."

"I did not slay anyone, nor command that anyone be slain. Now your land is preserved, and the people yield to you. I have converted all the chieftains who submitted to me with their champions to Christ. The others I rejected, because they would not do so. I myself am such a Christian that I have vowed that, henceforth, I will never have the company of a wife. Now find me a successor, so that I may serve God in true devotion, as I have promised the Almighty."

The emperor embraced the champion of God and told him how his daughters served the Lord. Later, his two sisters also believed. Then, greatly rejoicing, they went to the hall and the holy Helena[17] arrived with the aforesaid maidens. They remained in chastity, leading a glorious way of life, until they departed from the world to Christ.

Afterward, Gallicanus freed five thousand people, and enriched them with possessions. To the poor, he distributed his numerous riches. He went away to a certain holy man, who was called Hilarianus, with some of his men who would not leave him. Four pieces of his own lands he gave away to strangers as defenses and as gifts to the poor.

Word spread widely throughout the land about how the great man washed people's feet, carried water for their hands, and served them food. He became so holy that he healed the sick and, as soon as he looked at them, insane people would be cleansed of unclean spirits.

Later, the cruel adversary Julian was chosen as emperor, even though he had been tonsured as a priest. Since he was so full of malice, he established a ban on the Christians owning anything in the world.

He exiled Gallicanus, that man of God, who journeyed to Alexandria, the city of the Egyptians. Then, he went into the desert and was a hermit, until a certain idol-worshiper slew him there, because he would not sacrifice to the foul gods. Thus, he journeyed in victory to Christ.

Julian, that same adversary, still wanted the holy brothers John and Paul to submit to his idolatry. But, when he could not entice those great servants of God into his household, nor persuade them to his idolatry, he sent one particular heathen man called Terentianus to them. With him, he had a single golden idol.

"Our Lord Julian has commanded that you pray to this idol, or I will slay both of you," he said to these men of God.

"We do not know any God, except the Father and the Son and the Holy Ghost," the saints replied. "Your lord has forsaken this holy Trinity, and wants to convince others into ruin with him."

So, Terentianus commanded that the two brothers be beheaded and secretly buried in their house.

Soon afterward, through St Mary's bidding, Julian was slain for his bloodthirstiness and Christianity thrived. The saints became evident, since insane people were healed in the same house in which

---

17 Helena is Constantine's mother. She was revered as a saint throughout late antiquity and the Middle Ages for her search to find the cross on which Christ was crucified. The Old English poem *Elene* commemorates her discovery of the relics of the Holy Cross.

those saints lay. When Terentianus' son, who was filled with a dark devil, ran to their tombs in a horrible rage. Immediately his father sought the tombs. He confessed his sin that he had slain the saints. Then, he became baptized and his son grew reasonable. Let it be praise to the Savior, who lives always in eternity. AMEN.

Cecilia

Beginning in the fifth century, Saint Cecilia became one of the most venerated saints of the Middle Ages. By emphasizing Cecilia's chastity within marriage, conventionally known as the *intactam sponsa* topos, this saint's legend offered medieval women a more practical possibility for achieving sanctity than the violence and refusal to marry presented in many other virgin martyrs' lives. Little historical evidence exists for the story of Cecilia, but an early Christian of this name was buried in the Catacomb of Callistus in Rome adjoining an ancient crypt of the popes. This evidence suggests that Cecilia probably lived during the last quarter of the second century or the first half of the third century. Although some early confusion existed concerning the date of her martyrdom, by the Middle Ages, her feast day was most commonly celebrated on November 22. Like Agatha, Agnes, Eugenia, and Lucy, Cecilia is classified as a virgin martyr.

The earliest evidence for the veneration of Cecilia's cult shows that the saint was commemorated in the fourth century, as attested by a fourth-century church in the Trastevere quarter of Rome dedicated to Saint Cecilia. Tradition has it that this church, still preserved, is located on property Cecilia or her family owned. It is possibly even part of her house mentioned in the legend. The mention of her name in five different masses affirms that the cult of Cecilia had become widely known by the end of the fifth century. During the fifth century, the *Life of St Cecilia* first appears in both Latin[1] and Greek versions. The Latin legend of Cecilia is found throughout medieval Europe in more than forty manuscripts dated before 1100. Her name also appears in many martyrologies and religious calendars from this period.[2]

In Anglo-Saxon England, knowledge of Cecilia's story circulated widely from the earliest periods. In the late seventh or early eighth-century, Aldhelm praises her and Bede includes her in his poem in praise of virginity.[3] Brief versions of her legend are included

---

[1] Mombrizio 1, pp. 332–41; BHL 1495–1500.
[2] These include Ado, Florus, Hieronymian, Hrabanus, and Lyons.
[3] Bede, chapter IV, book 20.

in both Bede's eighth-century martyrology and in the anonymous ninth-century *Old English Martyrology*. Her name also appears in twenty-two religious calendars[4] and forty-five Anglo-Saxon litanies dated before 1100. Four English churches also were dedicated to this saint prior to 1700. Her life appears in one pre-1100 Anglo-Saxon manuscript other than the base manuscript used for this translation.

Life of Saint Cecilia

In ancient times, during the Roman Empire when the cruel persecution was performed in the days of the emperors who did not care for Christ, there was one particular maiden called Cecilia, who was a Christian from childhood. This holy young woman had such a great love for the eternal life in her heart that she thought about the Gospel of the Lord and about the teachings of God, day and night. She occupied herself constantly with prayers and with faith. However, since her relatives wished it, she was married to a noble retainer, called Valerian, who was not then a Christian, but who is now a holy saint.

So, Cecilia clothed her own body in haircloth. She fasted often and prayed, weeping, that she would be shielded from any defilement or intercourse with a man. She called upon the saints and the high angels, begging for their aid from Heavenly God that she be allowed to serve Christ in purity.

Even so, it came to pass that the worthy retainer carried out the bridal ceremony, and took that maiden for worldly honor as befitted their rank.

Among the songs and the constant rejoicing, always Cecilia sang to God.

"Fiat cor meum et corpus meum immaculatem, ut non confundar (Be my heart and my body undefiled through God, so that I not be disgraced)," she sang continually.

When they were brought to bed together, at once that wise maiden Cecilia spoke to her bridegroom. She taught about God, saying, "Oh you, my beloved man, I tell you in love that I have an angel of God who preserves me. If you defile me, he will immediately turn against you, and strike you in anger until you do not live. If you love and live with me in chastity, pure without disgrace, then Christ will love you, and He will reveal His grace to you as to me."

---

[4]   These are MCR, twenty from Wormald, and St Willibrord's calendar.

The retainer became frightened and said to the maiden, "Make it so that I might see the angel for myself, if you want me to believe your words about it. If another retainer is more intimate with you than I, then I will kill him and you together."

"If you believe in Christ, and are baptized from former sins, you will be able to see the shining angel immediately," Cecilia said.

"Who can baptize me suddenly, so that I can see this shining angel?" Valerian replied.

The woman instructed the retainer for a long time, until he believed in the living God. Afterward, he traveled to the pope, called Urban,[5] who was very near there, and begged him for baptism.

The pope rejoiced that he had been converted to God. As was his custom, he prayed to the Almighty God that he direct the retainer, until he became a believer.

Even then, suddenly before their eyes, an angel of God appeared with a single, golden book. When Valerian fell to the ground frightened, the angel raised him up, commanding that he read the golden letters which God had sent. In the book, these words were inscribed, "Unus deus, una fides, unum baptisma (There is one Almighty God, and one faith, and one baptism)."[6]

After he accepted the reading, the angel said, "Do you believe this, or would something else please you?"

"What could ever be more truthful or as believable to anyone living?" Valerian answered.

At these words, the angel departed from them. At once, the pope baptized him, and taught him his faith.

When he was allowed to travel home again to the holy maiden Cecilia, the retainer found the woman standing in her room alone at her prayers. An angel of God with golden wings and two royal crowns was standing near the maiden.

Wonderfully, the royal crowns shone with the redness of a rose and the whiteness of a lily.[7] He gave one to the noble maiden and the other to the retainer, saying to them, "Keep these royal crowns with a pure heart. Because I received them in Paradise, they will never wither, nor lose their sweetness, nor will their beautiful appearance

---

5   There was an historical Urban, apparently an early bishop and confessor, who died in c.230.

6   Ephesians 4:5.

7   In *Spiritual Marriage: Sexual Abstinence in Medieval Wedlock* (Princeton: Princeton University Press, 1993), Dyan Elliott notes of these floral crowns that roses and lilies are "well known symbols of martyrdom which also evoke classical marriage rites, which involve double crowning of the bride and groom," p. 69.

lessen. No one can see them, except someone who loves purity. Since you love purity, Valerian, the Savior commands you to request whatever you want."

The retainer kneeled and said to the angel, "There is nothing so beloved to me in this life than my brother. It is difficult for me to think that I might be redeemed, but he will be lost in torments. This request I ask, that my brother Tiburtius be redeemed and converted to the faith, and that He would make both of us His worshipers."

"Because you have asked for this," the angel replied with joy, "God is well pleased. Your brother Tiburtius will be born into eternal life through you, even as you have believed in God through Cecilia's teaching. And you two, both you and your brother, will be martyred together."

Then, the angel went up to Heaven.

In bliss, they deliberated and spoke gladly about God's will, until his brother arrived in the morning. With joy, he kissed them both and said, "On a winter day, I wonder why there is such a delightful and sweet smell of a lily's blossom or the fragrance of a rose here. Even if I had the blossoms in my hands, they would not give so sweet a fragrance. I say that I am filled truly with such a sweet fragrance, it is as if I were revived."

"At my request, this sweet fragrance comes to you," his brother said, "so that afterward you would know whose blood reddens like a rose and whose body is as fair as a whitened lily. We have holy crowns on us, as shining as a rose and as snow-white as a lily. Although they are shining, you cannot see these."

"Tell me, my brother, am I hearing this in my sleep or are you saying it in earnest?" Tiburtius asked.

"Until this, we lived as if we were asleep," the other said to him, "but now we are converted to truthfulness. The gods whom we worshiped are cruel devils."

"How do you know that?" said the other.

Valerian answered, "An angel of God taught me. Indeed, you might see him, if you would be cleansed from foul devil-worship by baptism."

For a long time, they spoke, until he was converted to the faith.

When his brother wanted him to be baptized, Tiburtius asked who should baptize him.

"The Pope Urban," the other said.

"He is outlawed and travels in secret because of his Christianity," Tiburtius responded. "If we go to him, we will be punished, if it becomes known. It is said that if we follow his teachings, we will find trouble and lifelessness on earth, even though we sought divine nature in Heaven."

At once, Cecilia said boldly, "If this life were the only one, and another was not better, then we could rightly dread our death."

"Is there any other life?" Tiburtius asked.

"Every man knows," Cecilia said to him, "that this life is full of labor and we live in sweat. This life will be borne in long-lasting pain. It will be dried up by heat, weakened by hunger, filled with meat, exalted by wealth, destroyed by poverty, uplifted by youth, bowed by old age, broken by sickness, overwhelmed by grief, and afflicted with anxiety. When death comes, it will take all the joy we enjoyed in his life from memory. But, in the eternal life, that comes after this, rest and joy will be granted to the righteous, and eternal tortures to the unrighteous."

"Who has come to this side from there?" Tiburtius asked. "Who can tell us if it is so?"

Cecilia rose up then, and said firmly, "The Creator of all beings begat one Son, and He brought forth from himself the Comforting Spirit. Through the Son, He formed all creatures and quickened them through the Living Spirit."

"You preach one God, but now you have named three individual gods," Tiburtius answered.

Cecilia replied to him, "There is one God Almighty, dwelling in His majesty. We Christians always worship Him in Trinity as well as in true unity, since the Father, Son, and the Comforting Spirit have one nature and one kingdom, just as there are actually three things in a single person; sense, will, and memory, always together serving one person."

Tiburtius fell frightened at her knees. In faith, he cried out, "To me, you do not seem to speak in human speech. It is as though an angel of God himself speaks through you! But I ask again about the other life. Who has seen it and has come here afterward?"

Wisely, Cecilia answered him, telling how the Savior came to us from Heaven, of the many miracles He wrought in this world, how He raised the dead from death into life, how He himself rose from death on the third day, and many other things she plainly told him about Christ.

Then, Tiburtius wept and sincerely wished that he be baptized by the aforesaid Pope. Immediately, his brother traveled forth with him, and revealed to the Pope what they had said.

Rejoicing in God, the Pope Urban baptized the fortunate retainer at once. Continuously for seven days, he told him about the faith, until he had traveled completely back again. From God, he received spiritual blessings, so that every day he saw the angels of God. Whatever he wanted, God would not refuse him. Through him and his brother, the books say He often wrought miracles.

In the city of Rome, there was a certain harsh executioner, called Almachius, who was the prefect. When he could learn about them, he martyred the Christians with many tortures, and would not allow anyone to bury them. Until the wicked persecutor learned of their deeds, Valerian and his aforesaid brother buried the martyrs, whom the cruel one had killed, and they contributed gifts daily to the needy.

Then Almachius commanded that those men be summoned. With harsh threats, he immediately asked them why they buried those who had scorned his orders and lay slain for their offenses, and why they secretly distributed their possessions to lowly people because of foolish advice.

When Tiburtius answered the cruel one, he said, "Oh, if those saints whom you commanded be slain and whom we buried, would have us as the least servants in their service!"

They pleaded for a long time, until the cruel one commanded that the other brother be beaten with clubs.

Then, one particular advisor said to the fierce one, "Sire, command that they be killed, since they are Christians. If you delay now, they will distribute their wealth to the needy and the destitute. You may punish them later, but because of your delay you will not have their wealth."

Almachius ordered his harsh executioners to lead the brothers in bonds together to the heathen temple. He commanded that they sacrifice or else instantly one would slay them with a sword.

As the harsh one commanded, Maximus, along with other executioners, brought them to the place of execution. Since they wanted to perish, Maximus wept. He asked the brothers why they went to their own deaths as joyfully as if to a banquet.[8]

"We would not hurry toward death in such great bliss," the older brother said, "if, as we have learned, we were not going to an even better life. We will be slain for the eternal life."

As they were hurried forth during these teachings, this Maximus

---

[8] This common theme of torture or death being welcomed can also be found in Agatha's *Life,* which similarly describes the saint going joyfully into her prison as if to a banquet.

said to the martyrs, "I would also renounce the enticements of this world, if I knew for certain that your words were true."

"Our Lord Christ will make it happen that when we are slain, you will behold how our souls journey to Him with glory," the younger brother said to him from his bonds, "if you promise now that you will repent your sins with all your heart."

"May fire consume me, if I do not convert to Christ once I see how your souls travel to the other life you speak about," Maximus said to the martyrs.

The holy brothers, whom he led in bonds, said, "Until you can be baptized from former sins, command now these executioners to hold us alive in your own house for this one night, so that you will be able to see the vision from God."

In bonds, they were led to his house and the blessed Cecilia came there at once with venerable priests. That night, they sat speaking about Christ, until the executioners believed and were baptized by the aforesaid priests.

At daybreak, that precious maiden Cecilia called out to them all, "Champions of God, promptly cast away from you the work of darkness, and with weapons of light be girded now for this struggle![9] You have fought a very good battle. During your life's course, you have fulfilled and preserved the faith. For the crown of glory, which the righteous judge will give you as a reward, go to the pleasant life."

Then, for their faith, they were led to slaughter and beheaded with a sword. Maximus watched.

"Truly, when they were slain," he said to those bystanders with an oath, "I saw angels of God, shining like the sun, flying to them, and they took their souls! On the wings of those angels, I saw the souls travel very radiantly to Heaven."

With weeping eyes, Maximus said these words so sincerely that many heathens were converted to the faith from their lying gods.

When Almachius discovered that the honorable Maximus with all his household believed in the Savior, and that they had been baptized, he became angry at him and commanded that he be scourged with lead whips, until he departed from the world to Christ.

Soon after, Cecilia buried the saint in a stone tomb there on the same site in which the two brothers[10] had been buried before. She then secretly contributed her bridegroom's wealth and his brother's things to the poor.

---

[9] Romans 13:12.
[10] All three martyrs are buried in the Roman cemetery of Praetextatus.

Since she was a widow, Almachius wanted to know about the wealth and she was forced to sacrifice to the base gods. The heathens wept that a woman so beautiful, noble, and filled with wisdom, should suffer death from tortures so young.

Cecilia spoke to them all, "He who lies slain for God will not be abandoned. Through death, he will be changed to glory. It is as if a man would sell dirt and receive gold for himself, as if he would give up a common house, but receive a glorious one. So, he would give up the transitory and receive the permanent, give a base stone and get a worthy gem."

She taught the unbelieving heathens for a long while, until they all said in unison, "We believe that Christ, the Son of God, is truly God, and has accepted you as His handmaid in the world."

Four hundred people were then baptized in Cecilia's house in praise to the Savior. In that same house, the pope frequently celebrated mass for the people, and heathenship declined because of that.

Then, the wicked Almachius commanded that the blessed Cecilia be fetched quickly. He immediately asked about her family. For a long time, they conversed, until the judge wearied of her insolence.

"Don't you know my power?" he said scornfully to the maiden.

"Since you command me," the maiden said, "I will tell what kind of power you have: The power of every man who goes in arrogance. It is as though a man would sew up a flask and blow it full of wind. When it has swelled up in its greatness, a hole develops and its power goes away."

As they fought with words, Almachius said to her, "Unfortunate one, don't you know that I have the authority to slaughter and to revive? So boldly you speak reproaching my power!"

"Arrogance is one thing, firmness is another," the maiden replied. "Because we avoid arrogance entirely, I speak with firmness, but not arrogantly."

Further, she said to him, "You said you have the authority to quench life and to revive it. I say that since you can only destroy the living, but cannot give life to the dead again, you plainly lie."

"Cast aside your insolence and offer an honorable sacrifice to the gods!" Almachius answered.

"Test by touching whether those whom you call gods are stones and stony idols, covered with lead," Cecilia said to him. "If you cannot see that they are stones, you can know for certain by touching. If anyone put them on a fire heap, they would be good mortar. Now, if anyone put them onto a fire, they would be as mortar and could benefit neither themselves nor people."

At once, the wicked judge grew fiendishly angry, commanding her to be led to her own house, and boiled in water in the name of the Savior. When the heathens did as Almachius commanded them, with her body unharmed she lay for more than a day and night, in the bath above the burning fire, as though she were in cold water, so that she did not even sweat.

They revealed to Almachius how in the hot bath that maiden remained whole in body and without even sweating. At this, he sent an executioner to her, and commanded that she be beheaded in the hot water. The executioner struck her with his sword, once, and again, and a third time, but her neck was unbroken. He left her lying half dead, since the senators had said that, when slaying a guilty person, no executioner should strike anyone four times.

For three days, she lived and taught the faithful. Then, she entrusted her maidens to the illustrious pope, and her house became consecrated as a holy church. Through God, miracles frequently happened there. The Pope Urban buried her honorably for the glory of the Almighty who rules always in eternity. AMEN.

Eugenia

S aint Eugenia's story is one of the most popular of the female transvestite saints' legends that circulated in Western Europe and Eastern Christendom in the early Middle Ages. The hagiographic subgroup of transvestite saints recounts the lives of women who cross-dressed as men in religious contexts. Twenty-three stories of such female transvestite saints circulated throughout medieval Europe prior to 1050 when the Old English version of Eugenia's life was copied into the manuscript used here. Her story, along with that of Euphrosyne, also translated in this collection, are the only holy transvestite saints' narratives surviving in Old English.

While we know little about the historical authenticity of the events related in Eugenia's life, records indicate that a Christian by this name was martyred in Rome in the first half of the third century. Other documents from this time also record a Philippus who held an official position similar to those ascribed to them in this text. Considered one of the virgin martyrs, her feast day is most commonly celebrated on December 25. An alternate tradition from Greek sources, however, celebrates her martyrdom on December 24.

Beyond these few facts, we know only that this saint's story attracted popular interest shortly after her death, as inscriptions from monuments and iconographical evidence attest. As early as the late fifth century, Eugenia's cult had gained widespread recognition in Western Europe and the Near East. Her story is mentioned by Avitus, who died in 518, and in the early sixth-century monastic rule, the *Regula Magisteri*, which even quotes from her life. Her earliest narrative biography is a Latin text,[1] taken from a slightly earlier Greek text,[2] that dates from the fifth century. Her story is recorded in poetry by Venantius Fortunatus and in a litany of elegiac couplets composed by Hrabanus. A lengthy portion of the ninth-century Carolingian work *De Triumphis Christi*, by Flodoard of Rheims, also venerates the saint.[3] Many medieval Latin martyrologies also include this saint

---

[1] PL 21:1105–1122; BHL 2666.

[2] BHG 607–608.

[3] Flodoard's text may be found in PL 135:491–886.

in their lists.[4] By 1100, at least twenty-five manuscripts of one version of this saint's life had been copied into Latin manuscripts.

In Anglo-Saxon England, Eugenia's legend was widely known from early in the region's Christian history. Eugenia is mentioned in religious calendars and martyrologies,[5] as well as in nineteen litanies from Anglo-Saxon England before 1100. Further evidence of her story's early appeal to Anglo-Saxon religious communities may be found in Aldhelm's late seventh- or early eighth-century Anglo-Latin adaptation of the legend in his *Carmen de Virginitate*. Redactions of her legend also appear in at least two important Latin manuscripts from Anglo-Saxon England. The text translated here is Ælfric's only holy biography of a transvestite saint.

Life of Saint Eugenia

Anyone who wants may hear how that holy maiden Eugenia, Philippus' daughter, thrived gloriously through her virginity and through martyrdom triumphed over this earth.

There was a certain highborn noble called Philippus. The emperor Commodus, who ruled in those days, sent him from the city of Rome to the city called Alexandria and appointed him prefect over Alexandria and the land of the Egyptians. Because the nobleman Philippus had never been baptized to God, he commanded him to uphold Roman law, since Christianity was not yet known everywhere and the cruel persecution of it had not yet ceased.[6] His wife was named Claudia, by whom he conceived two sons, Avitus and Sergius, and one daughter, Eugenia, about whom we speak.

Her father Philippus promised that she would be educated in worldly wisdom and taught Greek philosophy and Latin eloquence. Eugenia, that noble maiden, progressed so well in wisdom and philosophy that when the teaching of that holy apostle Paul, the great teacher of all mankind, later came into her hand, her mind became greatly inspired by that holy teaching, even though she was still a pagan.

After this, because she wanted to seek out the teachings of these

---

4   Among these are Ado, Florus, Hieronymian, Hrabanus, Lyons, and Usuard.

5   These include Bede's *Martyrology*, OEM, and ten calendars in Wormald.

6   The explanation that Philippus was not baptized because Christianity had not yet spread throughout the world appears in the Old English version of the legend, but not in the original Latin source.

Christians, she asked her father to allow her to journey throughout his home in the district of Alexandria. Since Philippus had previously expelled all the Christians from Alexandria, there was in the city no faithful person who knew their teachings.

Rapidly, Eugenia journeyed, until she came to where the Christians were singing with great joy. Celebrating God, they sang thus, "Omnes dii gentium demonia; dominus autem caelos fecit (All the pagan gods are devils, and the Lord truly wrought the heavens)."[7] Eugenia immediately was strongly affected. Weeping, she spoke to her two servants, whose names were Protus and Jacinctus. They had been educated in Latin and Greek with Eugenia about worldly knowledge. They were eunuchs (that is, they had been castrated), and they were loyal and true to their lady.

Eugenia took them aside to speak privately. She called them brothers, asked that they cut off her hair in the custom of males,[8] and through garments pretend that she was a young man. Because she did not want to be revealed, she wanted to draw near the Christians in a masculine guise.

These three left their traveling companions, and journeyed until they came to the Christians' dwellings, where day and night they praised their Lord.

On that same day, a certain bishop of the holy life called Helenus arrived with a great multitude, all singing together, "Uia iustorum recta facta est, et iter sanctorum preparata est (The way of the righteous is laid straight, and the footpath of the holy is prepared)."[9] This bishop wrought many miracles through God. While he slept, everything in this maiden's heart was made clear to him.

During this time, that maiden spoke to a certain masspriest, called Eutropius, asking him to relay a message to the bishop for her in these earnest words: "We three brothers desire to turn from the base pagan religion to the Savior Christ, and we never want to be separated."

In the morning, after the masspriest relayed the maiden's words to the illustrious bishop, the bishop commanded them to be summoned,

---

7   Psalms 96:5.

8   The Old English word translated here as *males* is *wæpmonna*, literally meaning *weapon-bearing men*. While such a term could mean simply adult men who bear arms, immediately following its occurrence is the word *cniht*, a term that can, in this context, suggest a male youth. Because of this, as well as the Old English text's general tendency to play with gender-specific language, it seems likely that *wæpmonna* is meant to evoke phallic connotations.

9   Isaiah 26:7.

thanking the Almighty God that He had wanted to disclose the maiden's desire to him. He took her aside, telling her that she was not truly a man, but was a maiden, whose virginity greatly pleased the Heavenly King she had chosen. He told her that she would endure severe persecutions because of her virginity, but still she would be shielded by the true Lord, who shields His chosen ones.

To her two servants, he said that they should keep a noble purpose in mind, although they served men. He said that Christ would have spoken these Gospel words to them: "I command you never as servants, but as my friends."[10] The bishop ordered that the converted maiden remain in her masculine disguise until they had been purified in the baptismal font and secretly had joined the monastic way of life.

Although she was a maiden, Eugenia then dwelled in the monastery in a male habit. With her two servants, unknown to anyone, she maintained a holy way of life in her customs. She satisfied the Savior through the kindness of her spirit, great humility, and holy virtues. With God's will, she prospered in the teachings of the true faith and the divine writings. She was changed from a wolf into a sheep. Her servants, Protus and Jacinctus, also modeled her sequestered way of life and completely hid her secret.

During this time, her father Philippus grieved in his heart, and her mother Claudia was seized with mourning. Distressed in their spirits, all her family searched for the maiden with great sorrow. They asked witches, wise druids, and also their lying gods, about the handmaid of God. It was told to them, as if it were a true fact, that the gods had snatched her because of her goodness. Her father believed the lies and commanded that a statue of her be forged from pure gold. Even though it was only gold, he worshiped it as if it were a holy goddess.

Three years after she had been converted, her master the abbot died. At once, the brethren acted to choose Eugenia as abbot because of her pious life. They still did not know she was a woman. That maiden grew extremely concerned about how she would ever be able to guide men. However, since she did not dare disturb them all by rejecting their counsel, she accepted the office.

By her exceedingly good behavior in God's service, Eugenia set an example for them all, and guided that community with care. Any ailing people she visited who were in pain, the Almighty Ruler

---

[10] John 15:15.

allowed her to heal. By means of her true faith, she also expelled foul devils from any afflicted people.

There was one woman, particularly wealthy in possessions, named Melantia, who was extremely tormented with a long-lasting fever. When she came to the young woman, Eugenia smeared her with hallowed oil and marked her with the sign of the cross.[11] Afterward, she spewed out all the cruel poison that harmed her, and was healed by that holy maiden.

In return for her healing, the widow offered the maiden treasures, but, for the sake of true reward, she refused them, charging the other woman to donate them to the needy and the poor.

After the widow had returned home to her properties, she often came to the beautiful maiden, whom she believed was a young man, with deceptive intentions. Constantly, she offered her abundant treasures. But, when she saw that the trustworthy young woman was interested neither in her gifts nor her charms, she became completely filled with evil.

Pretending she was ill for a shameful purpose, she asked Eugenia to visit her, and tried to tell her black thoughts to her. She said she had become a widow that year, and that her husband had left behind "not a few possessions in land, livestock, and household-servants. In this life, there was no man[12] who came between us two. But, my heart now turns strongly to you, so that you would master these possessions and me. If you enjoyed a woman and happiness in life, I believe it would not be wrong to God."

In answer to this temptation, Eugenia told the woman this insight, "Even though they might be pleasant, the longings of this temporal world are highly deceptive, and often the lusts of the body seduce and lead into sorrow those who love them most strongly."[13]

After this advice and other teachings, the prostitute embraced that untainted maiden and wanted to subject her to shameful intercourse.

Eugenia blessed herself. To the scandalous woman, she said that she was truly "an inferno of lust and a kinswoman of demons, a companion of darkness and filled with blackness, a daughter of Death

---

[11] Although the Latin text notes that Eugenia marked Melantia with oil, it never mentions that this mark included the sign of the cross.

[12] While some have translated the Old English term *man* here as *sin*, its alternate meaning of *male person* is more in keeping here with Melantia's efforts to seduce the man (Eugenia) who she insists has turned her desires away from her deceased husband.

[13] II Corinthians 4:18.

and vessel for a Devil! Let those who are like you have your posses-sions. We have all things in the Almighty Lord!"

Melantia became very ashamed. Since she thought Eugenia would reveal her words unless she first made it publicly known, she jour-neyed quickly to the city of Alexandria. She began to accuse her and sought to slander her to the governor, called Philippus, who was Eugenia's father, although the foul woman did not know it.

She said that Eugenia had come to her sickbed in the guise of a doctor and wanted her to commit adultery, if she would bear that shame: "But, at once with a dreadful scream, I cried out, so that one of my women rescued me from him."

Philippus believed the sinful story. Furious, he commanded that Eugenia be seized and that the brothers also be bound. In a window-less prison, he held them captive, until he could revenge that woman through torture.

When the day came that the judge had appointed, those innocent Christians were brought before the judge in black chains. They were prepared for cruel tortures. Enraged, Philippus said to his own daughter, Eugenia, "Wicked one, tell us why you wanted to seduce that illustrious woman Melantia with wantonness, and wanted to commit adultery with her in the guise of a doctor."

Eugenia said that, if Philippus would assure by a firm oath that the lying accuser would not be condemned, she easily could clear herself of the dishonor of this adultery and refute Melantia's story with truth. Philippus swore he would protect the lying widow, even if she were forsworn.

Then, Eugenia asked that the female slave be obliged to tell the judge how it had happened, and how she had rescued her lady from her lusts.

The prefect also commanded that the male servants, Melantia's household workers, reveal anything they had heard about this.

The female slave said she knew how, at one time, Eugenia had basely set out to engage in adultery, and had wanted finally to shame her lady. But she shouted out hastily to her: "These men of the house-hold, whom I called here, know this."

The men of the household said it was true. Under oath, they all lied about Eugenia. The prefect grew extremely angry. He asked Eugenia how she alone might refute all those witnesses under oath or through any kind of sign absolve herself.

Then, Eugenia, the noble young woman, said that to keep her purity only for Christ, she had wanted to hide herself by dwelling in virginity unknown to humankind. Therefore, from the beginning she had taken up the clothes of a man's rank and had been tonsured.

After these words, she tore open her clothes and revealed her breasts to the famous Philippus. She said to him, "You are my father and your wife,[14] Claudia, bore me to humankind. These sitting beside you are my brothers, Avitus and Sergius. I am truly called Eugenia, your own daughter. For Christ's love, I left all of you, and scorned earthly desires[15] as if they were dung.[16] Also here are those servants, your foster-children Protus and Jacinctus, to whom I made known my secret. With them, I came to Christ's school where I have conducted myself until this very day, and I will always serve them until the end."

Then, they recognized Eugenia, Philippus as her father, and Avitus and Sergius as their own sister, and their household servants kissed them humbly. At once, this was revealed to Claudia, her mother. In utter joy, she came to Eugenia, overwhelmed with wonder. To Eugenia's displeasure, they adorned the young woman with gold and set her up beside them. At that, the people cried out that Christ was a true God. Afterward, with glory, they all praised the Savior.

So that she would not be punished by torture for her vicious persecution, earlier Eugenia had interceded with her beloved father for the lying Melantia. But, for everyone to see, Christ himself sent a roaring fire to Melantia's castle from Heaven above. It burned everything, until nothing of hers was left.

Once Philippus, Claudia, and their two sons were baptized to the true faith, a multitude of people converted to Christ's practices. These enriched the Christians.

For eight years, the abandoned churches were restored and the faith grew. Then, Philippus sent to the emperor Severus. He said that the Christians strongly supported his kingdom and the Roman nation, and that they were so well esteemed they should dwell without persecution in the same city from which he had expelled them earlier. When the emperor granted the prefect this, the city of Alexandria soon became filled with much Christianity and many churches. In each of the cities, the Christians rejoiced and worshiped God in honor. Also abandoning heresy because of this, the Egyptian people believed in the Ruler. Philippus gave the Christians great wealth to use among themselves and watched over them.

Afterward, the lying heathens accused Philippus to the aforesaid

---

14 The Old English term here, *gebædda*, translates literally as *female bed-companion*.
15 Philippians 3:8.
16 As in the lives of Agnes and Agatha, this passage reflects the convention of the woman saint's scorn of worldly possessions as if they were dung.

emperor. They said he had abandoned the living gods and had converted all the citizens to Christ. Immediately, the emperor became irate and ordered that Philippus himself bow to his gods or he would be deprived of his position and possessions. Philippus secretly then distributed his possessions among all the district's churches and the needy.[17] Through great faith, he strengthened so many others that the Christians chose him as bishop.

After twelve months, the emperor remembered what he had been told. With a harsh order, he sent another prefect from Rome. He commanded him to kill the Christian Philippus if what had been said about him were true. Because of their friendship, when this prefect came, he dared not kill him with these people as witnesses.

Instead, he sent some men, who said they believed in Christ even though they lied, into the church. With great treachery, these struck down the illustrious bishop at his prayers. But, despite his wounds, he stayed alive for three days and comforted the Christians. Then, in martyrdom, he departed to the living Ruler whom he had worshiped in life.

Earlier, through her great devotion, Eugenia had founded a monastery of religious women, and her mother Claudia greatly endowed it. They buried the bishop Philippus there.

Afterward, all of them, the mother and daughter, along with the brothers, Sergius and Avitus, journeyed together to the illustrious city of Rome where, because of their former knowledge of the noble Philippus, the Roman senators received them well. At once, the senators appointed the young men to high positions in two chief cities, one in Africa and the other in Carthage. Eugenia dwelled in Rome. Because of her example, she converted many maidens to Christ, who lived in chastity because of her advice.

At that time, in the city of Rome, there was a certain royally born maiden, called Basilla, living in the heathen religion. She wanted to hear the holy teachings from Eugenia's mouth, but she could not go near her because Christianity was detested there. So Eugenia sent the two saints, Protus and Jacinctus, to the heathen maiden.

In bliss, Basilla received them and practiced God's teachings day and night with those precious saints. She did not cease her prayers, until Cornelius, bishop of the Christians, privately baptized her from all corruption. After that, the beloved maidens, Eugenia and Basilla, and also the bishop, were often much occupied in private speech. At

[17] In the Latin source, Philippus not only distributes his wealth, but also pretends to be ill.

night, they visited frequently, and with the holy bishop secretly held their religious rites.

Because of these two maidens, many others came to the faith of Christ and to a pure way of life. Because of Claudia, chaste widows with good wills also came to the faith of God, and many servants believed in Christ, because of the two saints, Protus and Jacinctus.

Basilla had one very noble heathen suitor, named Pompeius, to whom the emperor granted that royally-born maiden. But, since she had chosen Christ as her bridegroom, she would not have this heathen suitor. Because of this, the young man, with tearful pleadings, sought the feet of the emperor and the Roman senators. They spoke with him and agreed that the maidens, Eugenia and Basilla, should be obliged to petition for his support.

The emperor pronounced that Basilla should submit to the young man or she would be hewn in two with a sharp sword. He commanded that Eugenia make an offering to his gods or she would be killed by vicious tortures. He also commanded that all the Christians would be killed, if they would not submit to the shameful heathen religion. Since Basilla would choose no one as a bridegroom except Christ, whom she had already chosen, she was martyred for her virginity at home in her house with a sharp sword.

After these words, the two saints of God, Protus and Jacinctus, were immediately captured. They were required to offer their sacrifices to the gods or they themselves would be offered to them. When they were led to the loathsome idol of a goddess,[18] as soon as the saints prayed to God against her, she immediately fell down, crumbling at their feet. The judge said they had cast down the idols with sorcery and grew angry. He then commanded that these holy witnesses be beheaded. So, in victory, they journeyed to Christ. In life, these martyrs had never been defiled by a woman. Instead, with great faith, they had lived chastely until the end of their lives.

Afterward, the faithful Eugenia was captured. Under duress, she was brought to the heathen temple, in order to offer God's honor to the goddess Diana. When Eugenia herself prayed to the Almighty God, that devil's temple fell to the ground and, with all its idols, sank into the earth.[19]

---

[18] Although in the Old English text this idol is that of an unnamed female goddess, the Latin source identifies the deity as the male Roman god Jove.

[19] While the Old English description is vague, the Latin text states that an earthquake occurred. If this omission is original to the Old English text, it may have been altered because the inhabitants of the British Isles had no experience with such a phenomenon.

The emperor commanded that a single hewn stone be hung upon her holy neck and that she be shoved into the river.[20] But, the stone burst apart and she sat up on the water, so that the Christians would know that Christ was with her,[21] He who who once had led Saint Peter by the hand upon the high ocean, so that the waves of the sea could not swallow him.

Next, the emperor commanded that she be shoved into a burning oven, where the hot baths were. But, she quenched that fire and cooled the baths, completely extinguishing the conflagration when it came toward her.

Then, she was brought into a windowless prison. In that darkness for twenty days,[22] she was not allowed any nourishment. But, in a heavenly light, the Savior came and brought the maiden a snow-white loaf. That glorious nourishment illuminated the prison.

During this time, the Savior said to the holy maiden, "Eugenia, be not afraid. I am your Savior, whom you worship so highly, and love with all your heart and strength. On the day that I came to human-kind, you shall come to me. On my birthday, you will be brought into Heaven."

On the day of Christ's nativity, the executioner sent by the emperor came and killed that maiden. She was martyred and the Christian people buried her.

Later, with great sorrow, her mother wept at her tomb,[23] until she saw her in a spiritual vision, adorned with gold among a heavenly host.[24]

"My mother Claudia," she comforted her, "my Savior Christ has brought me into the bliss of His saints and has lodged my father among the patriarchs' number. Now on Sunday, you will come to us."

---

[20] The Latin source identifies this river as the Tiber and the location of Eugenia's torture as the island of Lyconia.

[21] In the Latin source, it is Peter, not Christ, who accompanies Eugenia on the water. By making its reference to Peter parenthetical, the Old English text re-instates the original biblical locus of this scene.

[22] In the Latin text, Eugenia is incarcerated for only ten days.

[23] The Latin text records that Eugenia's tomb was located on her own property (pre-sumably the convent she founded) on the Via Latina.

[24] The description of the virgin saint returning adorned in gold in a vision to a member of her family is a common hagiographical convention, which is also found in the *Life of St Agnes*.

On that Sunday, the mother departed from the world into Heaven, while her sons Sergius and Avitus stood by her. After this, they remained true in the faith until the end of their lives. Let there be glory and praise to the benevolent Lord for all His beneficence always and forever.[25] AMEN.

---

[25] Although literally translated as something like "always in the world of all worlds," the Old English term *ealra worulda woruld ealra* is commonly translated in the sense of *forever and ever*, as in the phrase, *per omnia secula saeculorum*, commonly used in Latin liturgical texts.

Euphrosyne

Another female transvestite saint's legend, the story of Saint Euphrosyne circulated widely in Eastern Christendom, but was less popular in Western Europe during the early Middle Ages. Together with the *Life of St Eugenia*, Euphrosyne's holy biography is one of only two holy transvestite saints' narratives surviving in an Old English version. However, unlike the active martyr Eugenia, Euphrosyne led a life of ascetic contemplation and, like Saint Mary of Egypt and Saint Æthelthryth, was not martyred. Euphrosyne's status as a virgin saint is due largely to her impressive devotion to her faith and to the miracles her body and relics invoked after her death.

Little is known about any historical figure on whom Euphrosyne's life may have been based. Surviving versions of her legend never record the names of any historical persons found in official documents from late antiquity and, since she was not martyred, her death does not appear in any legal records. Modern scholarship accepts that, if this account is not wholly fictionalized, the saint most likely lived during the fifth century. Her feast day is commonly recorded as February 11, although some early texts celebrate her death on January 1.

While her cult seems to have never achieved the widespread popularity of the other women saints' cults translated here, Euphrosyne's story was important enough to be included in several of the most important eighth- and early ninth-century Latin martyrologies.[1] The earliest complete version of Euphrosyne's life appears in Greek sources[2] dated to the seventh century. The Latin text,[3] on which the anonymous Old English text translated here is based, is from the eighth century. At least eleven Latin manuscripts, dated before 1100, containing Euphrosyne's life have survived from Western Europe.

In Anglo-Saxon England, knowledge of Euphrosyne's story is mentioned as early as the eighth century in Bede's *Martyrology*, a text compiled not long after the earliest versions of her life appear in

---

[1] These include the martyrologies of Ado, Florus, Lyons, Notker, and Usuard.

[2] PL 131:1029–1164; BHG 625–26.

[3] PL 73:643–52; BHL 2723.

Latin. Her name is also included in two litanies from Anglo-Saxon manuscripts copied before 1100. In addition to the Old English manuscript used for this collection, Euphrosyne's life appears before 1100 in one other manuscript from Anglo-Saxon England. The Old English text translated here appears in a manuscript that contains works largely attributed to Ælfric, but stylistic evidence supports the argument that the *Life of St Euphrosyne* was not written by Ælfric.[4] The rise in popularity of her cult after 1050[5] suggests that the tenth-century Benedictine reform movement in England may have encouraged renewed interest in her cult because of the highly ascetic type of devotion her life advocates.

Life of Saint Euphrosyne

In the province of Alexandria, there was a certain man named Paphnuntius, who was loved and honored by all people. Earnestly, he observed God's commandments. He took for himself a companion equal to his own rank, who was filled with all the worthy virtues, except that she was barren. Since there was no child between them who could receive his possessions when he had passed away, this was very troubling to her husband.

Daily, she dispensed her riches to the needy.[6] She also frequently visited church. In supplication she prayed to God that he might grant them a child, especially because she knew her husband's sorrow.

He himself journeyed throughout many religious places, hoping he might find some person of God who could aid him in his desire.

At last, he came to a particular monastery, where the father of the monastery was greatly esteemed by God. When he gave a large sum of money to this place, he received much companionship from the abbot and from the brethren. After awhile, he told his desire to the abbot. The abbot sympathized with him, and earnestly prayed to God

---

4   In his article, "The Chronology of Ælfric's Works," Peter A.M. Clemoes presented evidence that the *Life of St Euphrosyne* in the *Lives of Saints* collection was not written by Ælfric. For a useful review of the stylistic features of this and the other anonymous texts included in this manuscript, see Hugh Magennis, "Contrasting Features in the Non-Ælfrician Lives in the Old English *Lives of Saints*," *Anglia* 104.3–4 (1986): 116–48.

5   At least sixty manuscripts from Western Europe and England attest to a lively interest in Euphrosyne's cult after 1100.

6   In the Latin source, it is the husband, Paphnuntius, rather than his wife, who distributes money to the poor.

that He grant the nobleman the fruit of a child. Then, God heard the prayers of them both, and granted him one daughter.

Once Paphnuntius had seen the abbot's glorious way of life, he seldom left the monastery. In order for her to receive the blessings of the abbot and the brethren, he also brought his wife with him to the monastery. When the child was seven years old, they baptized her and named her Euphrosyne.[7] Because she had been accepted by God and was so beautiful in appearance, her parents were extremely happy for her.

When she was twelve years old, her mother died. Afterward, her father educated the maiden in holy writings, religious readings, and all worldly wisdom. So deeply did she understand those teachings that her father marveled greatly at it. Her fame, wisdom, and learning spread throughout the entire city.

Because she was adorned with such virtues, many people became so enthralled with her that they sought her in lawful marriage and spoke to her father about it. He always responded, "May God's will be done."

Finally, one noble, wealthier and more worthy than all the others, came to him, wanting her for himself. Promising her to him, her father accepted his dowry.

After some time, when she was eighteen years old, her father took her with him to the holy place he visited. As usual, he gave a great sum of money to that place.

"Because I want to give her to a man, I have brought my daughter here, the fruit of your prayers, so that you might give her your blessing," he said to the abbot.

The abbot ordered that she be led to the chapterhouse. For a long time, he spoke with her, teaching her about purity, patience, and fear of God. She stayed there for seven days, attentively listening to the brothers' songs and observing their conduct. Marveling greatly at all this, she said, "Blessed are these men who are like angels in this world. Because of it, they achieve eternal life."

Afterward, she grew thoughtful about them.

On the third day,[8] Paphnuntius said to the abbot, "Go, father, so

---

7 Although the form used in the Old English text is *Eufrosina*, I have used the more common Latin form of this name. *Euphrosyne*, or the alternative spelling *Euphrosyna*, is used in most scholarship concerning this saint.

8 There is a problem of time here. A few lines earlier the text states that Euphrosyne stayed seven days in the monastery, but here it is three days.

that your handmaid might greet you, and receive your blessing, because we want to travel home."

When the abbot came, she fell at his feet and said, "Father, pray for me, so that God might secure my soul for himself."

The abbot extended his hand and blessed her, saying, "Lord God, You who knew Adam before he was created, may You deem that You should care for this handmaid of Yours, so that she might partake in the heavenly kingdom."

After these words, they journeyed home.

It was Paphnuntius' custom that whenever any monk came to him, he would bring him into his house and ask that he bless his daughter. About a year later, when it was the abbot's ordination day, he sent a brother to Paphnuntius to invite him to the celebration.

When the monk came to his hall, he did not find him at home. Since Euphrosyne knew the monk was there, she called him to her and said, "Tell me, brother, for the sake of true love, how many of you are in the monastery?"

"Three hundred and fifty-two monks," he replied.

She asked further, saying, "If anyone wants to dwell there, will your abbot take him in?"

"Yes," said he, "and most of all because of the Lord's command that says thus, 'he who comes to me, I will not drive him away from me.' "[9]

"Do you all sing in church individually?" she asked."And do you all fast in the same way?"

The brother answered, "We sing all together in unison, but each of us fasts according to what seems appropriate to him. In order that none of us be in disagreement with holy conduct, each should do what he chooses willingly."[10]

When she had contemplated everything about their behavior, she said, "I want to convert to such a way of life, but I fear that I would be disobedient to my father who, because of his useless riches, wants me to be married to a man."

"Oh, sister!" the brother said. "Don't permit anyone to defile your body, nor should you soil your beauty with any shame. Wed yourself to Christ, who can give the heavenly kingdom in return for these

---

[9]   John 6:37.

[10] A similar statement about monastic practices is made with reference to the monks in Zosimus' community in the *Life of St Mary of Egypt*. Since both monasteries are said to be near Alexandria, this may reflect common practices in monastic communities of the region.

transitory things. Now journey in secret to a monastery. Lay aside your worldly clothes also, and clothe yourself in a monk's robe, so that you will escape notice most easily."

This speech pleased her, but she then asked, "But who can cut my hair? I would not wish those who have no belief in God to do it."

"Look, your father will go with me to the monastery, and he will remain there for three or four days. In the meantime, send for one of our brethren. Any one of them will gladly come to you."

As this was happening, Paphnuntius came home. When he saw the monk, he asked him why he had come. He told him that it was going to be the abbot's ordination day, and that he should come with him for his blessing. Quite happily, Paphnuntius journeyed with him to the monastery.

Euphrosyne then sent a certain servant, who was extremely loyal to her, to the monastery. She asked that whichever monk he found within the church, "Bring him to me."

Through God's mercy, he met one of the monks outside the monastery. The servant asked him to come with him to Euphrosyne.

When he came to her, she greeted him and said, "Pray for me." He prayed for her, blessed her, and sat with her.

"Lord," she said to him, "I have a Christian father, who is a true servant of God. He has many possessions. His spouse, my mother, has departed from this life. Because of his useless riches, my father now wants to give me to a man. Although I don't want myself to be tainted by that, I dare not be disobedient to my father. I don't know what I can do about this. Truly, all this night I have remained alone, praying to God that He might show His mercy to my poor soul. At daybreak, it seemed right to me that I get one of your own to come to me, so that I might hear God's word from him. For your soul's reward, I pray that you guide me in the things that are suitable to God."

The brother replied, "The Lord said in His Gospel, 'whoever does not forsake father and mother and all his relatives, and thereby improves his own soul, cannot be my disciple.'[11] I do not know what more I can say to you. Unless you can conquer the temptations of the flesh, leave all that you own and depart from here, your father's possessions will find a young heir."

"So that I might achieve the salvation of my soul, I will trust in God's help, and in you," the maiden said.

[11] Luke 14:26.

The brother said, "You should not allow such a desire to slacken. Indeed, you know that now is the time for repentance."

"I invited you here," she replied, "because I wanted you to bless me and then shear off my hair."

The brother clothed her in a monk's robe and blessed her, saying thus, "May the Lord, who redeemed the saints, preserve you from all evil."

In bliss, he journeyed home, praising God.

Euphrosyne thought about this, saying, "If I journeyed now to a monastery for women, my father would seek me and find me there. Then, he would take me by force for my bridegroom's sake. So, I will journey to a monastery for men where no one would expect me."

Then, she took off her womanly attire and clothed herself as a man. In the evening, she departed from her hall and took fifty silver coins[12] with her. That night, she hid herself in a secret place.

On the morning after that, Paphnuntius came to the city and, according to God's will, went into the church. Meanwhile, Euphrosyne arrived at the monastery her father visited.

The gatekeeper went to the abbot and said to him, "Father, a eunuch has come here from a king's household. He wants conversation with you."

The abbot went outside. Immediately, she fell at his feet. When she had received his blessing, they sat together. After this, the abbot said, "Child, for what purpose have you come here?"

"I was in a king's household, and I am a eunuch," she answered. "I have always wanted to convert to a monastic life, but such a life is not usual in our city. I have learned of your exalted way of life and, if it be your will, my desire is that I be allowed to live with you. I have abundant riches and, if God would grant me rest here, I will bring it about that they be brought here."

The abbot said, "Welcome to you, my child! Indeed, this is our monastery. Dwell here with us, if it pleases you."

When he inquired of him[13] what his name might be, he said, "I am called Smaragdus."

"You are young," the abbot said to him. "You cannot live alone. It

---

[12] Since no appropriate modern English equivalent exists for the Old English term *mancsas*, I have translated this term more freely as *silver coins*.

[13] At this point in the text, the writer begins to use masculine pronouns to refer to Euphrosyne. This unusual shift in pronouns suggests either that the reader is meant to see the saint as a viewer in the text would (i.e., the male monks) or that Euphrosyne's male disguise is indicative of an inward, more permanent spiritual transformation.

will be necessary for you to have someone who can teach you monastic conduct and the holy rule."

"I will do, my father, as you say," he replied.

Next, he drew out the fifty silver pieces and gave them to the abbot, saying, "Father, take this money without delay. If I stay here, the remainder will be brought here."

Then, the abbot called a certain brother named Agapitus, a person of the holy life and worthy in virtues. He entrusted the aforementioned Smaragdus to him and said, "From now on, this shall be your son and your pupil."

Afterward, Agapitus took him to his cell.

Because Smaragdus was so beautiful in appearance, the accursed spirit would send continual thoughts into their minds. Whenever the brothers came to the church, they became sorely tempted by Smaragdus' fairness.

At last, when they had all grown disturbed with the abbot because he had brought such a beautiful man into their monastery, he called Smaragdus to him and said, "My child, your appearance is beautiful and will bring much ruin to these brothers because of their frailties. From now on, I want you to stay by yourself in your cell. Sing your hours there and eat by yourself there. Also, I don't want you to go anywhere else."

He commanded that Agapitus prepare an empty cell and bring Smaragdus into it. Agapitus completed what the abbot had ordered. He brought Smaragdus to the deserted cell, where he occupied himself day and night with fastings and vigils, serving God with such a pure heart that his teacher marveled greatly about him and related his conduct to the brethren.

When her true father Paphnuntius came home, he quickly went to the room in which his daughter usually stayed. But, when he did not find her there, he became terribly unhappy and tried to discover from all the free servants what had happened to his daughter Euphrosyne.

They said, "Last night we saw her, but this morning we did not know where she had gone. We thought that her bridegroom, whom she was to marry, might have taken her from here."

So he sent to the bridegroom and asked for her there. But she was not there.

When her bridegroom heard that she was lost, he became very upset. He came to Paphnuntius and found him lying grief-stricken on the ground. Later, since some people said that perhaps someone had deceived her and led her away, he sent people riding all throughout the land of Alexandria and Egypt. They looked for her among sailors, in a women's monastery, in deserts, in caves, and at the houses of all their usual friends and neighbors. When they could not find her anywhere, they wept for her as if she were dead.

The father-in-law mourned his daughter-in-law and the bridegroom his bride. The father wept for his daughter and said, "Woe me, my sweetest child! Woe me, light of my eyes and comfort of my life! Who has deprived me of my riches or has destroyed my possessions? Who has cut down my vineyard or extinguished my torch? Who has parted me from my joy or has stained the beauty of my daughter? What wolf has captured my lamb or what place on sea or land has hidden a face so royal? In grief, she was a comfort, and a rest for affliction. Oh, Earth, you will never swallow my blood, until I have seen what has happened to my daughter Euphrosyne!"

Upon hearing these words, they all began to weep, and there was much wailing throughout the city. Since Paphnuntius could find no tranquility nor receive any comfort, he journeyed to the abbot. He fell at his feet, saying, "I beg you not to stop praying for me, until I might discover the result of your prayers. Indeed, I do not know where my daughter has gone."

When the abbot heard this, he became extremely unhappy. He commanded all the brothers to gather around him and said, "Let us now show our friend true love. Let us pray together to God, until He decides to show him what has happened to his daughter."

All week they fasted and remained in their prayers, but no sign came to them, even though this was unusual when they prayed for anything.

Indeed, day and night, the prayer to God of the blessed young woman Euphrosyne was that she would never be discovered during the course of her life.

When no sign came to the abbot and the brethren, he consoled Paphnuntius by saying, "Child, don't give up because of the Lord's rejection. He labors on behalf of every child He loves. Know that without God's will a single sparrow does not fall to the earth.[14] How can anything very significant have happened to your daughter without God's intention? Since nothing was revealed to us about her, I know she has chosen some good plan for herself. If it were, far be it, that your daughter had slipped into any harm, God would not ignore the work of these brothers. So, I trust in God that He will yet reveal her in this life."

---

[14] Luke 12:6–7.

Encouraged by these words, he journeyed home, praising God, and then busied himself in good deeds and charities.

One day, he returned to the abbot and said, "Pray for me, because my pain has increased more and more in me because of my sorrow for my daughter."

Sympathizing with him, the abbot said, "Would you like to speak with a certain brother who came from the household of King Theodosius?"

Since he did not know she was his daughter, he readily said that he would. The abbot then commanded Agapitus to bring him to the brother Smaragdus.

When she looked on her father, she became overwhelmed with tears. Because she had become excessively thin from her extreme and strict way of life, he assumed it was from excitement and never recognized her.[15] She also covered her head with her cowl, so that he would not know her.

After finishing their prayers, they sat together. She then began to speak to him about the blessedness of the kingdom of Heaven, how the entrance is gained with charitable deeds and other innumerable good works,[16] and that a person should not love father and mother and other worldly things above God. She told him the apostolic saying that tribulation builds patience and that he would be so tested.[17]

She said again, "Believe me, God will never forsake you. If your daughter had fallen into any harm, God would make it known to you. Therefore, she has not been lost. So, trust in God that she has chosen some good plan for herself. Give up your great suffering. Agapitus, my teacher, explained to me how sorely distressed you are about your daughter, and how you asked the abbot and his brothers for help. Now, even though I am weak and sinful, I myself will also pray to God that He might give you patience and perseverance, and grant you that which is best for you and most suitable for her. So that you might find some comfort in my humility, I would like to see you often."

Then, she said, "Go now, my lord."

---

[15] The Latin source is even more specific about the reasons Paphnuntius does not recognize his daughter. It records that her appearance had changed, not only because she was thin from excessive fasting and her hood covered her face, but also because she was coughing up blood.

[16] In the Latin source, humility, chastity, and religious conversion, along with charity and good works, are listed as practices for achieving salvation.

[17] Romans 5:3–4.

Greatly strengthened by her reassurances, Paphnuntius departed from her.

He went to the abbot and said to him, "My heart has been strengthened by this brother, and I am as glad as if I had found my daughter."

Then, he commended the abbot and the brethren for their intercession on his behalf and journeyed home, praising God.

When Smaragdus had remained unknown in that state for thirty-eight years, he was struck down by illness, and he passed away because of it.[18]

At that time, Paphnuntius came again to the monastery. After speaking to the abbot and brothers, he asked to be allowed to go to Smaragdus. The abbot commanded that he be brought there.

Paphnuntius sat with him as he was ill and, weeping, said to him, "Woe me! Where is the promise you promised me that I would be able to see my daughter again? Just now, we had some comfort through you, but you will abandon us. Woe me! Who shall console my old age? To whom shall I go that will help me? My pain is doubled. It is thirty-eight years now since my daughter was lost to me. Although I eagerly yearned for it, no sign ever came to me. Unbearable sorrow holds me. Whom may I cherish henceforth or from whom may I receive such comfort? Thus, in total mourning, I will descend into Hell."

When Smaragdus saw he would not accept any comfort, he said to him, "Why are you so terribly distressed, and why do you want to kill yourself? Do you say that the Lord's hand is weak or that anything might be difficult for Him? Now put an end to your distress and remember how God revealed to the patriarch Jacob his son Joseph, whom he also mourned as if he were dead. So I ask that you not leave me for three days."

During these three days, Paphnuntius considered this, saying to himself, "Perhaps God has revealed to him something about me."

On the third day, he said to him, "I have waited, brother, these three days."

When, Smaragdus, who was previously called Euphrosyne, perceived that the day of her[19] death had come, she said to him, "God

---

[18] Since Euphrosyne continues to interact with her father after this statement, the comment that Euphrosyne has died at this point in the text should be taken as an anticipatory summation of what follows, rather than as reflective of sequentially occurring plot events.

[19] At this point in the text, the Old English redactor returns to using female pronouns to refer to Euphrosyne/Smaragdus.

Almighty has directed my poor life well and has fulfilled my desire that I be allowed to end the course of my life as a man. It was not accomplished through my might, but through the help of Him who preserved me from the fiend's cunning. Now, with my time ending, the path of righteousness holds a crown of glory for me."

"No longer should you be anxious about your daughter, Euphrosyne. Truly, I am her poor self, and you are my father Paphnuntius. Just now, you have seen me, and your yearning has been fulfilled. But, do not let anyone know about this, and do not permit any person to wash and prepare my body, except yourself. I also told the abbot that I had many possessions, and promised him that I would give them to this place, if I remained here. Grant what I have promised, because this place is worthy of the honor, and pray for me."

Having said this, she yielded up her spirit.

When Paphnuntius heard these words, and saw that she had died, all his limbs trembled, until he fell to the ground as if he were dead.

Agapitus ran in, saw the dead Smaragdus, and Paphnuntius lying half-alive on the ground. He threw water on him, lifted him up and said, "How are you, my lord?"

He replied, "Leave me here to die. Truly, I have seen the wonder of God today!"

Afterward, he arose and fell upon her weeping, saying thus: "Woe me! My sweetest child! Why would you not make yourself known to me, so that I might have lived with you of my own free will? Woe me! That you kept yourself secret for so long! How have you endured the cunning of the ancient fiend, but now go to the eternal life?"

Upon hearing this, Agapitus grew greatly astonished. Quickly, he went to the abbot and told him everything.

He came there and fell on the holy body, saying, "Euphrosyne, Christ's bride and offspring of holy people, you will not be forgotten by your fellow-servants and this monastery! Because He enables us to come as men to the harbor of salvation, pray to the Lord for us and enable us to share with Him and His saints."

When he commanded that the brethren gather together, and commit the holy body to a burial of honor, they discovered she was a woman. They glorified her to God, He who had worked such miracles in the womanly and delicate form.

At this time, one brother, who was blind in one eye, came there and, weeping, he kissed the holy corpse. When he touched her, his eye was restored to him.

So, they all praised God from whom all things come that are good. Then, they buried her in the tombs of the fathers.[20]

Later, her father gave a large portion of his riches to the monasteries and to God's churches. But, he was taken into that particular monastery with the greatest portion of his possessions.[21] He dwelled for ten years in the same cell in which his daughter had previously lived. He himself also practiced good conduct. When he departed to the Lord, the abbot and his congregation buried him with his daughter. The day of their death[22] is celebrated in the monastery until this present day. For God, the Father in glory, and for His only-born Son, our Lord Savior Christ, together with the Holy Spirit, let there be glory and honor forever and ever. AMEN.

[20] The Old English plural forms of the noun and definite article here indicate that the reference is to the graves of either the monastery's founding fathers or the succession of the monastery's abbots.

[21] While here the wealth belongs to Paphnuntius himself, the Latin source remarks that he gave what would have been Euphrosyne's inheritance to the monastery.

[22] Paphnuntius was also venerated after his death. His feast day falls on September 25.

Lucy

Although records are few and unreliable, Saint Lucy of Syracuse was probably born c.283 and martyred c.303, during the persecutions of Diocletian. Her father seems to have been Roman, but the name Euthycia suggests that Lucy's mother may have had Greek origins. Another of the saints classified as virgin martyrs, Lucy's feast day is celebrated on December 13. Her legend stems from the *Life of St Agatha*. In fact, the healing of Lucy's mother at Agatha's tomb provides not only the inspiration for Lucy's subsequent devotion to the Christian faith, but the miracle also supports and advances Agatha's cult's assertion of her transcendence into sainthood.

Early evidence for the cult of this saint appears in the canon of St Gregory I (c.540–604). She is one of the few female saints he mentions in this canon and in special prayers also recorded by St Gregory. The Latin text[1] for Lucy's life was composed in the late fifth century. A Greek text from the same period also survives.[2] Several early martyrologies[3] confirm the popularity of her cult. In the Middle Ages, Latin versions of the life of Lucy appear in at least forty-eight pre-1100 manuscripts from Western Europe.

In Anglo-Saxon England, the cult of Lucy appears in Bede's eighth-century martyrology and in the ninth-century *Old English Martyrology*. Aldhelm praises Lucy's devotion to her faith and her virginity in his *Carmen de Virginitate* from the late seventh or early eighth centuries. Forty-three litanies and twenty-one calendars[4] in Anglo-Saxon manuscripts dated before 1100, as well as two dedications from pre-1700 English churches, provide witnesses for her cult's popularity in Anglo-Saxon England. One Old English manuscript, other than the manuscript used for this translation, includes a pre-1100 version of Lucy's life. Her legend is also told in twelfth- and thirteenth-century Anglo-Norman versions.

---

[1] Mombrizio 2:58, BHL 4992–5003.
[2] BHG 995–96.
[3] Among these are Ado, Florus, Hieronymian, and Lyons.
[4] Hrabanus and twenty in Wormald.

Life of Saint Lucy

The fame of Agatha spread over land and sea, so that a great host from Syracuse, over fifty miles away, sought the tomb of this maiden in the city of Catania[5] with much excitement.

A widow named Euthycia came with the other people to the famous tomb. With her was her daughter, the blessed Lucy. The widow was unhealthy, because her blood had flowed for four years' time. Many physicians had tried to help her, but alone they were unsuccessful.

At the mass, someone happened to read in the Gospel about how a woman whose blood had flowed was healed when she touched the garment of the Savior.[6]

With faith, Lucy said to her mother, "If you believe in this famous Gospel, mother, believe that when Agatha suffered for Christ in His name, she earned that, in eternal bliss, she would be in his presence always. Touch her tomb, and you will be healed immediately."

After the mass, the mother and her daughter prostrated themselves in prayer before the tomb. Because they were lying down and the prayers were so long, Lucy fell asleep, and she saw Agatha, splendidly adorned in a company of angels.[7]

"My sister, Lucy, true maiden of God," she cried out to her from above, "why do you pray before me about this? You yourself could bestow it on your mother. Your holy faith has helped, and she is restored to health even now through Christ. As this city is made famous through me for Christ, so the city of Syracuse will become beautiful through you, because you have prepared for Christ a delightful dwelling in your pure maidenhood."

When Lucy awoke, she rose trembling because of the bright vision. To her mother, she said, "You are mightily healed. I ask you now, for the sake of the one who healed you by prayers, that you will never give me to any bridegroom nor seek any mortal offspring from my body. But those things which you would give me for defilement, give to me for purity, for going to Christ."

"You know my property," her mother said. "I have kept the property of your father for nine years now against all loss and have

---

[5] Catania is in Sicily.

[6] Matthew 9:20.

[7] Other examples of this common topos of women saints appearing in visions, splendidly adorned, appear in the lives of Agnes and Eugenia.

increased it further. First, close my eyes, and then distribute those riches however it might please you, my beloved daughter."

Lucy said, "Listen to my advice. You cannot take anything with you from this life. For the name of the Lord, what you might give in death, you should give now, because you cannot carry it away with you. Give now to the true Savior in prosperity, whatever you intend to give in death."

Lucy continued to urge her mother, until she sold her shining gems and landed property for ready money. Then, she donated it to the needy, to strangers, to widows, to the wretched, and to the wise servants of God.

This came to the attention of a noble youth, called Pascasius, a wicked idolater. He wooed Lucy and tried to persuade that holy maiden to sacrifice to the devils.

But, the maiden of the Lord said, "It is a sincere offering, pleasing to God, that someone should visit widows, console the wretched, and help orphans in their distress. I have not worked for three years now on any other deeds, in order to offer this sacrifice to the living Lord. I want to offer myself to Him now, because I no longer have anything I can spend on His sacrifice."

Pascasius grew enraged. They argued much, until he threatened that she would be whipped, if she would not be silent.

"The word of the living God cannot be refused or suppressed," Lucy said to him.

He asked then with contempt, "Are you a god, indeed?"

"I am a handmaid of the Almighty," Lucy answered, "and I have spoken the word of God. As He said in His Gospel 'It is not you who speaks there, but the Holy Ghost speaks in you.' "[8]

"The Holy Ghost dwells in you, truly?" Pascasius scornfully questioned her again.

Lucy answered the wicked one, saying, "The apostle promised those who preserved purity that they would be the temple of God and the dwelling of the Holy Ghost."[9]

Then, the wicked one said, "I order you to be taken quickly to the house of prostitutes, so that you will lose your maidenhood. The Holy Ghost will flee from you, when you have been completely disgraced."

Lucy answered, "The body cannot be dangerously defiled, if it does not please the mind. Although you may lift up my hand to your idolatry, and thus, through me sacrifice against my will, I will still be

[8] Mark 13:11.
[9] I Corinthians 6:18–19.

innocent before the true God, He who judges by the will and knows all things. If you defile me now without my will, my purity will be doubled and counted as a glory for me. You cannot bend my will to you. Whatever you might do to my body will not concern me."

The cruel one wanted his word carried out, so she was to be led to the loathsome debauchery. When they attempted to drag her into the lustful house, immediately the power of God was revealed in the maiden, since the Holy Ghost held her fastened with such weight that the evil ones could not move the maiden.

With cruel intent, they tied ropes to her hands and feet. Many pulled together, but she was unmoved and stood as if a mountain.

The wicked Pascasius grew anxious. He commanded that the lying magicians be summoned to him, so that they might overpower the maiden of God with their spells. But, it was no help to him.

Then, he commanded that oxen be attached, but even they could not move the maiden.

"What is the reason that a thousand men cannot stir you as weak as you are?" the executioner said to the pure maiden.

Lucy said, "Though you would call ten thousand men, they shall all hear the Holy Ghost saying thus 'Cadent a latere tuo mille, et decem millia a dextris tuis, tibi autem non adpropinquabit malum (A thousand will fall on your left and ten thousand on your right, but truly no evil will come near you).' "[10]

The wicked one again grew very anxious. He commanded that a great fire be kindled, encircling the maiden, and that she be spattered with pitch and sprinkled with oil.

She stood fearless in the fire, saying, "So that you will be shamed, I pray to Christ that this torturous fire will not subdue me, but will expel the fear of suffering from the faithful, and withhold evil joy from the unbelievers."

The cruel one grew furiously upset. Since his kinsmen could not endure his lack of courage, they commanded that the pure maiden be killed with a sword. Then, she was wounded so that her entrails flowed out. Even so she did not die, but was preserved by prayer as long as she wanted.

"I tell you as a truth," she said to the people, "that peace is granted to the congregation of God. The hostile emperor Diocletian is finished with his kingdom, and the wicked Maximianus is dead.[11] As

---

[10] Psalms 91:7.

[11] Lucy's prophecy that Maximianus would die immediately after Diocletian's reign ends does not accurately reflect historical events.

the city of Catania has inside its walls the great intercessions of my sister Agatha, so the Almighty God will allow me to intervene for you in this city of Syracuse, if you accept the faith."

As she spoke, the evil Pascasius, bound in chains, was led before the maiden. Earlier, because of his cruel deeds, he had been condemned by the Roman people, who ruled all that land. He was brought in bonds to Rome. Since he could not defend his crimes, the senators ordered that he be beheaded.

The blessed Lucy lived in that same place where she had been struck down, until the priests came to her and administered the sacrament with holy rites. She departed to Christ at the same time in which they said, "Amen." Afterward, the people raised a church where she had lain. In her name, they consecrated it to the Savior as a glory to God, who Himself rules always in eternity. AMEN.

Mary of Egypt

Like Mary Magdalene, Saint Mary of Egypt is one of the group of early saints known as the "holy harlots." In late antiquity and the Middle Ages, her story is even sometimes conflated with that of Mary Magdalene. However, since her story makes it clear that Mary of Egypt never took payment for her sexual encounters, the term "prostitute" can be applied to Mary of Egypt only in the broadest sense of a woman who offers her sexuality indiscriminately. The version of the legend translated in this collection is the only complete version of this or any other holy prostitute saint's life extant in Old English literature. It is also the only prose life of a non-virgin woman saint to survive in Old English.

While the legend's historical origins are as unclear as those of most early saints, particularly women saints, the death of the woman whose life provides the kernel for this story has been dated as early as c.421 and as late as c.549. Classified as a hermit or penitent saint, since she was neither a virgin nor a martyr, her feast day is meant to be celebrated as part of Lent, normally on the Thursday before Easter. But, Roman tradition commonly lists her feast day on either April 1 or 2. Following the account in her life more closely, Eastern tradition records her feast day on April 9. Also of note is that the Holy Sepulchre's prohibition of her initial attempts to enter is considered the first miracle of non-entry in Christian history.[1]

Although Mary of Egypt was commonly honored throughout Christian Europe and the Eastern Empire, her cult did not develop the same public popularity others enjoyed. Few martyrologies or religious calendars from early medieval Europe mention this saint. However, the *Life of Kyriakos*, written by Cyril of Scythopolis in c.560, includes the earliest mention of this saint's story. In the late sixth or early seventh century, Mary of Egypt's holy biography was written in Greek and became circulated widely throughout Eastern Christendom. This Greek text[2] is most often attributed to Sophronius of Jerusalem (d.638), although the accuracy of this attribution has

---

[1] See Benedicta Ward, *Miracles and the Medieval Mind: Theory, Record and Event 1000–1215* (London: Scolar Press, 1982), p. 123.

[2] PG 87 [3]: 3693–3726; BHG 1042.

been doubted. The Greek *Life of St Mary of Egypt* was translated into Latin by Paul the Deacon, probably in the second half of the eighth century. A ninth-century version of this text[3] rapidly became an extremely popular exemplar of repentance and redemption for medieval Christians. Because the Virgin Mary plays such a significant part in this saint's legend, medieval writers also sometimes included descriptions of Mary of Egypt's story in works related to the miracles of the Virgin. Numerous copies of the versions of this saint's life survive in continental manuscripts.[4] Although the Old English version here represents the oldest surviving vernacular translation of this saint's life, the primary Latin version of her legend appears in at least nineteen continental medieval manuscripts and in three surviving English manuscripts dated before 1100.

Along with the *Life of St Euphrosyne*, the Old English *Life of St Mary of Egypt* is one of four texts not written by Ælfric included in the base manuscript used for this translation. Written by an anonymous author at about the same time Ælfric wrote his texts, the Old English *Life of St Mary of Egypt* seldom condenses or reshapes the story for its audience, as is Ælfric's practice. Instead, the Old English version of this life translates the entire Latin text closely, in many places nearly word for word, preserving many of the Latin grammatical and syntactical structures of its source. While linguistic evidence suggests it may have earlier Anglian origins,[5] the text translated here is written in the West Saxon dialect of Old English. Since it is not included in the manuscript's list of contents and special arrangements were made to incorporate it into the manuscript,[6] it seems to have been a late addition to the manuscript. In fact, because it emphasizes a passive eremetical life of contemplative devotion rather than the actively heroic insistence on female chastity as a

---

3 PL 73: 671–90; BHL 5415.
4 In *Holy Women of Byzantium: Ten Saints' Lives in English Translation*, ed. Alice-Mary Talbot (Washington, DC: Dumbarton Oaks Center Studies, 1996), Maria Kouli records twenty-seven Greek manuscripts containing Mary of Egypt's life in the National Library of Athens and thirty-seven manuscripts of the Latin life in the Bibliothèque Nationale in Paris alone.
5 See Hugh Magennis, "St Mary of Egypt and Ælfric: Unlikely Bedfellows in Cotton Julius E.vii?" in *The Legend of Mary of Egypt in Medieval Insular Hagiography*, ed. Erich Pope and Bianca Ross (Dublin: Four Courts Press, 1996), p. 111.
6 For discussion of this, see Peter A.M. Clemoes, "The Chronology of Ælfric's Works" in *The Anglo-Saxons: Studies in Some Aspects of their History and Culture Presented to Bruce Dickens*, ed. Peter A.M. Clemoes (London: Bowes and Bowes, 1959), p. 219.

means to salvation that characterizes Ælfric's other women saints' lives, its inclusion in the Old English *Lives of Saints* manuscript has been considered contradictory to the focus of Ælfric's original compilation.[7] Although Mary of Egypt's story is not described in the *Old English Martyrology*, evidence for her cult's popularity in Anglo-Saxon England may be found in ten religious calendars dated prior to 1100.[8]

Life of Saint Mary of Egypt

This conversion, most commendable in both deeds and conduct, tells of the great penitence and brave struggle of the revered Mary the Egyptian. It is about how she in her lifetime was fulfilled in the desert, as is translated from the Greek language into Latin by Paul, the revered deacon of the church of the Saint Neapolis.

Indeed, it is explained that as Raphael the archangel was speaking to Tobit, after the loss of his eyes and their subsequent glorious illumination, as well as after the preceding dangers from which he had been rescued, he said thus:

"It is truly very dangerous that anyone might reveal the secret of a king,[9] and it also greatly distresses the soul that anyone should hide the glorious work of God.[10] For these reasons, I will not be quiet about anything regarding the holy histories. It has been revealed to me that I could fall into the condemnation told of the lazy servant, who accepted money from his lord, but concealed it in the earth, without increasing it.[11] So, let no one disbelieve me about what I have learned concerning the written matters. It will never happen that I misrepresent the holy histories, nor will I be silenced from speaking."

There was a particular man in a monastery in the country of Palestine. In his life's habits, he was extremely endowed, since from

---

[7] Hugh Magennis establishes a persuasive case for this argument in "St Mary of Egypt and Ælfric," pp. 99–112.

[8] These may be found in Wormald.

[9] The manuscript here reads *mancynnes*, a term that would normally be translated as *mankind*. However, since such a translation makes little sense in this context, I have taken *cynnes* in its alternate meaning of *royalty*. This reading not only makes more sense in this context, but also restores the original Latin sense of this passage.

[10] From the Apocryphal book of the Old Testament, Tobit 12:7.

[11] Matthew 25:14–30.

childhood he was highly skilled and learned in monastic customs. He was called Zosimus.

From the beginning, as I said before, this man lived in a certain monastery in Palestine, and among all the monastic practices he had become the most experienced in the discipline of temperance. All the orders of the rule and of monastic service he upheld perfectly and blamelessly. Also, he added upon himself practices besides those, because he wanted his flesh to be subjected to the spirit. He was so perfect in all monastic virtues that monks from far places and monasteries came to him quite often, in order to attach themselves to his example and to his teachings, and to subject themselves to the imitation of his temperance.

These disciplines he observed completely, and he never turned his mind from the contemplation of the Holy Scriptures. Because of all the goodness he practiced, he was satisfied in spirit. In one particular activity, he never restrained himself, that was in the glorious psalm-singing, nor did he ever weary in the contemplation of the Holy Scriptures.

As they have taught, he was also often made worthy to receive divine illumination from God through spiritual revelation, which is neither a miracle nor an unbelievable thing. Concerning this, the Lord himself had said, "Blessed be those who are pure in heart, because they will see God."[12] So much more clarity of divine illumination they will see, who continually purify their bodies through chaste virtues, and who with ever vigilant minds seek the future reward of eternal blessedness.

Zosimus told about himself that he had been entrusted to that monastery since he was born from his mother. He had lived in the rule there for fifty-three years, when he was struck by the thought that he might be perfect in all things and that his spirit no longer needed to learn from any example. He said, "Might there be any monk on earth who could teach me anything new, or help me in anything I myself do not know, or that I myself have not accomplished in monastic works? Or might any of those who love the desert be beyond me in his deeds?"

While he was thinking to himself about these and similar matters, there appeared next to him an angel, who said to him, "Oh, Zosimus! You have been very wonderfully fulfilled. Nevertheless, no one can show himself to be perfect. The struggle that is approaching you is much greater than that which has passed, though you do not know it.

12 Matthew 5:8.

For you to understand and know how remarkable other ways of salvation are, go out from your country and come to the monastery set near the Jordan."

Immediately, he traveled away from the monastery in which he had lived from childhood, and came to the Jordan, holiest of all the rivers. As the angel had commanded him, he went inside the monastery. First, he spoke with the monk, who guarded the gate of the monastery. Then he made himself known to the abbot, and was brought to him.

After the prayers that are customary for monks, the abbot said to him, "From where did you come, brother? Or why do you want to associate yourself with such humble-minded monks?"

"There is no need for me, father, to tell you from where I come," Zosimus answered. "But, I sought you here in order to learn, because I have heard of many spiritual practices here among you, which please God beyond expression."

The abbot said to him, "May God, who alone preserves and heals so many illnesses, strengthen you and us with His divine commands, and direct us to practice works that please Him. No one can instruct another, unless he constantly occupies himself, and works from strict knowledge of himself, with God as a witness. Nevertheless, because you, a humble-minded monk, have said that true love of Christ brought you to seek us here, live with us. If you have come for this reason, let the Good Shepherd feed us all together with the gift of the Holy Spirit."[13]

When the abbot had said these words, Zosimus kneeled. After praying, he dwelled in the monastery. He saw there, indeed, all manner of men who were brilliant in customs and deeds, burning ardently in the Spirit, and serving the Lord. Every day and at night, there was constant dedication to God's praise. Never were there any foolish speeches, nor thoughts of gold and silver, nor other treasures. Even the name of these was unknown among them. But, all of them especially strove for one thing alone; that each of them should be as if they were dead in body and living in spirit. Truly, because they were so unfailing, they had divine conversations. Their bodies were fed only with necessities, which were bread and water, so that for true love of God they might show themselves to be keener in these works. Zosimus eagerly observed this for himself and applied himself to perfection among his fellow-workers who, without ceasing, restored the sacred paradise.

[13] John 10:11–14.

After this, the time of the holy fast of Lent approached, which is arranged as a celebration for all Christian people and as a purification of themselves to worship the suffering of the Sacred One and His resurrection. The gate of the monastery was never opened, but was always locked, and thus they fulfilled their lives without any disruption. Nor was it ever opened, except perhaps when any monk would travel out for whatever might be necessary. The place was so isolated and secret that it was not only unfamiliar, but also even unknown, to the inhabitants of the country itself. From ancient times, the rule was kept this way, and it is believed that God brought Zosimus to that monastery because of these works.

Now, I will explain how the law of the monastery was kept on the Lord's Day of the first week of fasting, which we call Holy Day. The divine rites usually occurred, and then they partook of the communion of the living and undefiled body of our Lord Savior Christ. After this, they all ate together for awhile. Later, on bended knees and in humble prayers, they gathered in the chapel, greeting each other, and humbly begging their abbot for blessings, so that they grew more securely strengthened for the sacred struggle. When this had been accomplished, the monastery's gates were opened and together they sang this psalm, "Dominus illuminatio mea et salus mea, quem timebo."[14] Then, they went away together. They left one or two in the monastery, not because they wanted to guard the accumulated treasure, since there was so such thing there, but because they could not abandon the chapel without a sacred ritual.

Each of them supplied himself as he was able or as he wanted. Some carried with them an abundance for the body, some the apples of palm-trees, some beans moistened with water, some nothing except for their body and robes, so that they were fed by nature and necessity, obliged to rely on the vegetables that grew in the desert. So that none of them should know the ways or deeds of the others, each restrained himself with moderation as he thought suitable. Then, they would travel over the river Jordan. Afterward, each would separate himself from the others, and no one would come near his companions again. If any of them saw another coming toward him, he would immediately turn from his path, go in the opposite direction, and live by himself, keeping solitary prayers and fasts. When the fast had been completed, they would return again to the monastery before the day of Lord's resurrection, which would be the feast day we commonly call Palm Day. Within his own conscience, each of them had

---

[14] Psalms 27:1, "The Lord is my light and my salvation, of whom shall I fear?"

the witness of his own labor, for what he had toiled, and the seeds of the work which had been sown. None of them asked the others about how he had accomplished his struggle. Indeed, this was the rule of the monastery, and as I thus said earlier, in order to practice temperance, each drew near God by himself in the desert and struggled by himself, so that he might not please anyone, except God Himself.

Thus, because it was the usual law of the monastery, Zosimus traveled over the river Jordan. For the fame of the rule, he took very little with him for the necessity of his body. As he traveled through the desert, he ate a meal as the necessity of nature demanded. At night, he would sit on the earth and rest a little, and he would sleep wherever the nightfall met him. In the early morning, he would proceed again, determined to travel unceasingly. As he told afterward, he journeyed because he wanted to find a father in the desert, who could instruct him in matters he had not known before.

He continued that journey for twenty-six days,[15] as if he were traveling with certainty toward someone. Afterward, when midday came, he stopped for awhile, interrupting his own path, and went eastward. Since he was accustomed to pray at set times of the day's course to determine his path, he stood to sing and kneeled to pray. While he sang, he looked up and beheld the heavens with eager regard. Then, as he stood in prayer, a body appeared to him on his right side, in the semblance of a person. At first, he was extremely afraid, because he believed it was the spectre of some ghost he saw there. Nevertheless, he immediately bolstered himself with the sign of the cross, and so his fear was cast away. It was then that the goal of his prayer was also accomplished.

When he looked over, he saw someone there, hurrying westward into the desert. It was a woman whom he had seen there. She had a very dark body, because of the sun's heat, and the locks on her head were as white as wool and fell down no farther than her neck.[16] Earnestly, Zosimus watched where she went. Because of the sweetness of his desire for a glorious vision, he rejoiced and ran speedily

---

[15] In the Latin text, Zosimus travels for only twenty days.

[16] As Lynda L. Coon discusses in her recent study, *Sacred Fictions: Holy Women and Hagiography in Late Antiquity* (Philadelphia: University of Philadelphia Press, 1997), this description merges passages from the Old and New Testaments (Song of Solomon 1:5–6 and Revelation 1:14), illustrating "the paradoxical nature of late antique biographies of holy women" with its description of Mary as both light and dark, "a hideous wraith and at the same time the eschatological messiah; her body is repulsive yet she is the bride of Christ; she is a vessel of sin as well as of repentance," p. xiii.

in the direction that he had seen hurrying what he had been shown. In all the days before, he had seen no sight of humans, any forms of animals, birds, or wild beasts. Therefore, he ran eagerly, and wanted to know what that wild beast was which had been revealed to him.

As soon as Zosimus saw her, then truly he overcame his old age, and would not heed the effort of his journey. He ran, advancing with the swiftest course, because he wanted to connect with the one who escaped there. As he pursued her, she fled. Nevertheless, little by little, Zosimus ran closer to the stranger.

When he was so near that she could hear his voice, he began to send forth his voice in a loud cry. Weeping, he said, "You servant of God, why do you flee from me, an aged sinner? Wait for me, in the hope of reward for which you struggle so greatly! For the sake of God who casts no one away from him, stop and give me the blessing of your prayer!"

In tears, Zosimus uttered these words.

Running, she came to a certain place where there were signs of a dried-up stream. When they had come there, she shot into the stream and up again onto the other side.

Zosimus then called out again and again. There, on the other side of the stream that could be seen there, he stood, adding tears upon tears, and multiplying sighs with prolonged sighing, until nothing could be heard except the grief of his wailing.

After this, the body that had fled there sent forth this voice, which said, "You, abbot[17] Zosimus, have mercy on me! Because of God, I beg you. I cannot show myself to you and turn toward you because, as you might see for yourself, I am a female person, and am bereft of all covering for my body, and the shame of my body is uncovered. But if you would grant me, a miserable evil-doer, your redeeming prayers, then throw here the cloak in which you are wrapped, so that I can cover up my womanly frailty, and return to you to accept your prayers."

An intense fear and trembling gripped Zosimus, because he had heard her call him by name, although she had never seen nor ever heard tell of him before. Since he clearly perceived that she was enlightened by divine foresight, he calmly did as she had begged him. Unfastening the cloak in which he was covered, he turned his

---

17 The Latin text uses the term *abba*, a term of respect for an older person meaning *father*. Throughout the Old English text, however, the anonymous redactor seems to have confused this Latin word with the Old English term *abbod*, which can only mean *abbot*.

back and threw it to her. She took it,[18] and clothed her body, covering herself as best she could around that part which she had most need to hide.

Then, she turned to Zosimus and said, "Lo, abbot Zosimus, why did you have so great a need to see me, a sinful woman? Or what do you want to have from me or to know that would not allow you to slow in accomplishing such a great effort on my account?"

Immediately, he prostrated himself on the earth, and asked her blessing.

Asking his blessing, she then prostrated herself to him.

After several hours, the woman said to Zosimus, "It would be fitting for you, abbot Zosimus, to pray and bless, because you are endowed with the priestly teachings, and you have explained the gifts of the sacred sacraments of Christ, serving at the holy altar for many years."

These words brought much fear and trembling to Zosimus. He shook and became soaked with drops of sweat. He began to breathe hard, as if he had been totally weakened, and his breathing was choked when he said, "Oh you spiritual mother! Now grant me the insight of who you might be, because you are truly God's handmaid. You who are already as if dead, intercede for me now, for the sake of the younger portion of this world. But, most of all, for love of the divine, reveal how you called me by name whom you had never seen before. Since grace is not to be revealed by individual worth, but is measured instead by habitual deeds of the soul, bless me. For the Lord's sake, I beg you to grant me the prayer that I never be taken away from your perfection."

She began to sympathize with the steady old counselor and said, "God blesses him who tends to the salvation of the soul."

Answering "Amen," she then gave it[19] to Zosimus.

When they both rose from the earth, the woman began to speak again to the old man. She said, "Oh, man, for what reason have you come to me, a sinner? Perhaps the grace of the Holy Ghost has directed you so that you might provide a small service for my wretched body? Tell me how the people of Christ are governed today in the world, how the emperors are, and how the flock of Christ's righteous congregation is cared for now."

---

[18] After this point, parts of the manuscript London, BL, Cotton Julius E.vii become difficult to read. Therefore, to supplement the base manuscript and complete the text, I have supplied material found in the Latin text, edited by Stevenson.

[19] The blessing.

Zosimus answered her, "Oh you holy mother! Because of your holy prayers, God has granted a steadfast friendship. Thus, accept now the comfort of an unworthy monk. For the Lord's sake, pray for the world and for me, a sinful man, so that the effort of this path and the way through such a desert might not be useless to me."

"Abbot Zosimus, it would be appropriate for you to pray for me and for everyone because, as I said earlier, you are in the priesthood," she said. "But, for your sake, and because we have the commandment of obedience, I will do that which you commanded me with a good will."

Having said this, she turned to the east with her eyes raised up to the heights, and her arms uplifted. She began to pray, moving her lips in silence, so that no voice at all could have been distinguished by anyone.

Since Zosimus also could not distinguish anything of her prayers, he stood by himself, as he has said, trembling and looking at the earth, saying nothing at all. Indeed, with God as a witness to his words, he has sworn previously that while she remained persevering in such prayer, he raised his eyes for a little while from the earth, until he saw that she had been raised up by as much as the forearm of a man, and hung in the air above the earth while she prayed. When he saw this, he was seized with such a great fear that he prostrated himself on the earth, and became covered with sweat and extremely disturbed. He dared not say anything, except only to himself, "Lord, show mercy to me."

As he lay outstretched on the earth, he grew troubled, reflecting in his thoughts about whether it could be the appearance of some kind of ghost praying there. Then, the woman turned around and raised up the monk, saying, "Why do you trouble your thoughts, abbot, taking offense at me as if I were a ghost praying deceptively? But, know, man, that I am a sinful woman, even though I am externally endowed with holy baptism. I am not a ghost, but embers, dust, and all flesh, and I have no ghostly form."

When she had said thus, she blessed her face with the sign of the Holy Cross. Having fortified her eyes, lips, and breast with the blessing, she added, "God redeems us, abbot Zosimus, from our enemy and from his instigations, because his hatred for us is great."

Upon hearing these words, the old man prostrated himself and seized her feet. Speaking through tears, he said, "I call upon you, for the sake of the Lord Savior Christ, our true Lord who allowed Himself to be born from a virgin, for whose sake you have thus ruined your flesh, to hide nothing from your servant about who you are, and from where, and when, and for what reason you first came to live in this solitary place. Tell me everything about yourself, so that you might reveal the miraculous affairs of God. Because, as it is written, for what use is wisdom and treasure hidden?[20] Tell me everything, for the sake of God, because nothing you will say is because of boastfulness or pretentiousness, but instead it is meant to satisfy me, a sinner and unworthy. Since I trust God, for whom you live and with whom you have conversation, I was guided to this same desert, so that God might reveal these matters concerning you. It is not our authority to reject the decisions of God. If it were not pleasing to Christ to cause to reveal both you and your struggles, He would not have allowed you to be seen by anyone, nor would He have strengthened me, one who was not able to go anywhere nor was strong enough to walk outside of my room, to be able to make such a long journey."

As he spoke, saying other things also, the woman raised him up and said, "Pardon me, father, I am embarrassed for the sake of truth to tell you of the despicableness of my deeds. But, since you have seen my naked body, I will also expose the performance of my deeds to you, so that you will know how my soul is filled with vile lechery and corrupted by shame. As you yourself have perceived truly, I would not wish to relate matters about myself from any boastfulness, because what am I able to boast about, who became a vessel selected by the Devil himself? I know that if I explain these matters[21] about myself, in due time you will flee from me, as a man might flee a snake. Nevertheless, I will recount it to you, concealing nothing at all. But, first, I ask that you never stop praying for me, so that I might obtain some kind of mercy on the Day of Judgment."[22]

Overwhelmed by tears, the old man began to weep bitterly.

Afterward, the woman began to reveal and relate all the things that had happened to her, saying thus, "I had a brother, and a homeland in Egypt, and I lived there with my family. In my twelfth year, I began to reject their love, and came to the city of Alexandria. But, it shames me now to tell, from the beginning, how I first defiled my womanhood, and how constantly and insatiably I lay degraded in vices because of sinful lusts.

"This is the short explanation, indeed, but I would rather disclose

---

[20] Ecclesiastes 20:10.

[21] After this point, London, BL, Cotton Julius E.vii again provides a reliable text.

[22] Mary's reference to the Day of Judgment would have had particular significance to an Anglo-Saxon audience of the late tenth century, many of whom believed Judgment Day would arrive at the turn of the millennium.

it now, so that you might understand the illicit passion of my vices, which I had for the love of fornication. But, also pity me, abbot.

"For seventeen years, I clearly surpassed a great many people with a passion for fornication. I would never give my womanhood for any man's gift, nor receive as a gift any possessions from anyone. But I exceedingly craved the excitement of passion, so that I wanted them only to come to me in large numbers without payment. Because of this aim, I was able to satisfy the sinful longings of my promiscuity more easily. Do not think that I would accept any wealth but, as I said before, I always lived in poverty, because I had such insatiable desires that I myself continuously sullied in the filth of wicked intercourse. That was my misery and for me it counted as a life. So that I could practice this kind of wrong unceasingly, I lived thus.

"One particular summer, I saw a great multitude of Africans and Egyptians running together, as if toward the sea. When I met one of them by chance, I asked him where he thought the multitude was hurrying. He answered me, saying that they wanted to journey to Jerusalem for the glory of the Holy Cross, which would be worshiped not many days later.

"At this, I said to him, 'Do you know whether they would take me along if I wanted to travel with them?'

" 'If you have the passage money, none of them would prohibit you,' he said.

" 'Brother, I do not have any passage money to give,' I said to him. 'But, I want to go and set out on one of those ships. Even if they do not want it, they will feed me, and I will entrust myself to them. They may have control of my body for the passage money, so that they will take me immediately.'

"Have mercy on me, abbot, because I desired to travel with them in order to have workers in the service of my lusts! Since you don't need me to review my shamefulness, as I said before, show me mercy holy man. God knows I am afraid of these words of mine, because I know they will defile you or the air aloft!"

Soaking the earth with his tears, Zosimus said, "Oh spiritual mother, I beg you to tell it, for God's sake, and do not leave off the sequel of such a history of salvation."

So, she said, "At once, the young man understood the shame of my words, and he left me, laughing. At this, I cast away from me the spindle[23] I kept in my hands and I ran to the sea where I saw them

---

[23] Earlier, the Latin text explains that Mary supported herself by spinning flax threads, since she would not normally take money for her prostitution.

assembled. I saw ten young men standing together on the shore. They seemed sufficiently fair in body and in manner, and very pleasing for the cravings of my body. Shamelessly as usual, I mingled among them and told them, 'Take me with you on your journey. I will not be displeasing to you in any way.'

"Soon, I aroused them all with sinful vices, shameful jokes, and many other disgraceful and base conversations. Then, because of my immodest behavior, they sent me onto their ship with them and rowed forth.

"Oh, Zosimus, how can I explain to you, or in which tongue may I tell of, or hear with what ears, the sinful deeds that occurred on the voyage and were committed on the passage, and how I forced both willing wretches and paying wretches to transgress? There is no explanation, utterable or unutterable, for the baseness I enticed in the form and I taught to practice first. Now that you have observed this, I wonder how the sea endured, and suffered my wrongful lusts! Or why the earth did not open her mouth and sink me alive into Hell, which has brought so many souls into the snare of wantonness, unless I might hope that God sought my repentance, He who does not allow anyone to perish, but saves everyone who believes in Him, because He truly does not want the death of the sinful, but patiently waits for his conversion.[24]

"We traveled to Jerusalem in great haste and, for as many days as I had lived in the city before the Festival of the Cross, I engaged in works equally debased and even worse. I was never satisfied with the young men who had intercourse with me on the sea or on the passage. Instead I also gathered many foreigners and city-dwellers together, in order to exploit my vices, and I dishonored them by seduction.

"When the precious festival of the Exaltation of the Holy Cross[25] came, as I had done earlier, I went before the young men to apply the snare of wantonness. But, when I saw them all running in unison early in the morning to the church, I ran together with these runners, and tried to arrive with them in front of the temple.[26] When it was time to worship the Holy Cross, I violently began to press forward with the congregation and against the people. Through such struggle, unfortunately, I came to the door of the temple, with those going inside. I should have gone through the door, then, as each of them

---

[24] Ezekiel 18:23.
[25] This festival is commonly celebrated on September 14.
[26] The temple is commonly identified as the Temple of the Holy Sepulchre.

went through it without any hindrance. But, a sacred power prevented me from passing through the entrance. I was immediately crowded out from among all the people, until I was left standing alone in the courtyard.

"Afterward, I started to think this had happened to me because of my womanly weakness, and again I tried to mingle with the others, because I wanted to squeeze myself inside somehow. I labored in vain. As soon as I would touch the threshold of the door where they were all harbored inside without any hindrance, I alone was pushed out as if some strong host stood against me that wanted to halt my entrance. Thus, unexpectedly the punishment of God guarded the door from me, until I was standing again in the courtyard of the temple.

"Three or four times, I struggled to see, and to accomplish my desire. When I could not succeed, and my body was extremely tired from the pressure of the crowd, I seriously attempted to think it over. Then, I departed and stood by myself alone in a corner of the courtyard. In my mind, intently I pondered the faults prohibiting me from gaining access to the presence of the life-giving Tree. As I reflected within myself, my mind was inspired by knowledge of salvation, and the eyes of my heart urged me to think the entrance was locked on account of my unforgivable crimes.

"I began to weep bitterly. In great distress, I struck my breast and in painful sobbing, I brought forth lamentations from my innermost heart. Then, from where I stood, I saw an image of the Holy Mother of God standing there.[27] Without turning away, I looked at her intently, and said, 'Oh you, glorious lady, who gave birth in flesh to the true God long ago, I know it is not fitting nor so suitable that I, who am such a terrible miscreant, might behold your likeness, and that I, who am so vastly defiled, should pray for an insight. You are known to have been always a virgin, and your body has been pure and unstained. Because of this, it is right indeed that such a defiled

---

[27] The importance of the Virgin Mary within this text may suggest the reason for its inclusion in this manuscript that otherwise preserves texts which deal exclusively with virgins. In Anglo-Saxon England, the cult of the Virgin Mary developed early and had gained popularity in monastic circles by the late tenth century, at the same time the other women saints' lives here were written. Such a renewed interest in the cult of the Virgin Mary may have motivated the compilers of this manuscript to include this text. For a thorough discussion of the English development of this cult, see Mary Clayton's *The Cult of the Virgin Mary in Anglo-Saxon England*, Cambridge Studies in Anglo-Saxon England 2 (Cambridge: Cambridge University Press, 1990).

one as myself should be cut off, and cast away from your pure, unstained state. Nevertheless, I have heard that God was made human, because you bore Him yourself, so that He could summon the sinful to repentance.

" 'Now help me, who alone am deprived of any aid! Grant me leave to open the entrance of your holy church, so that I might not be alienated from the sight of the precious Cross on which the Savior of all the world was fastened, He whom you conceived as a virgin and whom you also bore as a virgin, He who shed His own blood for my redemption. Glorious lady, unworthy though I might be, command that the doors be unlocked, so that I might greet the Sacred Cross, and I will commit myself to you, and will choose you as a protector against your own child. I promise both of you that I will never again defile this body of mine by the fierce lust of sinful intercourse. Instead, Holy Virgin, as soon as I can see the Cross of your Son, I will forsake this world and its deeds, with all things in it, and will go afterward wherever you advise me as my protector.'

"Having said this, I was then fervently brought into belief and touched by the truth. Made daring by the compassion of the Mother of God, I stirred from the same place at which I had prayed," she said.[28]

"Again, I mingled with those going inside and then nothing could push me out or prevent me from entering the temple's door. As I went inside with those who were entering, a strong fear gripped me. I was completely distressed, and trembled when I came again to the door whose entrance had been locked to me earlier. This time, all that power, which before had prevented me from entering the door, had prepared the entrance for my path. Thus, inside the temple, I was filled with the spiritual mysteries, and deemed worthy to pray in the rites of the precious and life-giving Cross. When I saw the holy mysteries of God there, and how always He would accept the penitent, I cast myself forth onto the floor and kissed the holy earth.

"When I went outside again, I arrived at the place where before I had seen the likeness of the Holy Mother, and I kneeled before the holy statue in order to pray, saying these words, 'Oh you, beneficent lady, who has shown me your glorious mercy and would not cast my unworthy request away from you, I have seen that glory which we sinners might never see through our own efforts! Glory be to the Almighty God, He who accepts the repentance and atonement of

---

[28] The Old English *cwæð* here is the hagiographer's reminder to the audience that Mary is relating the story of her past to Zosimus in the present.

sinners and evil-doers. What can I, a miserable wretch, think to despair of or to explain more. Now it is time to complete what I said to you earlier. Because of your beneficial protection, care for me in whatever way you wish. Let a guide of salvation and a trustworthy leader be revealed to me now, to go before me along the way that leads to atonement.'

"As I spoke, I heard a voice calling from far away, saying 'If you would travel over the river Jordan, there you will find good rest.'

"When I heard this voice, I understood it had been summoned for my benefit. Weeping, I gazed upon the image of the Holy Mother of God, and cried out again, 'Oh, lady, you queen of all the world, through whom salvation came to all types of people, do not abandon me!'

"After saying this, I went out of the temple's courtyard and rapidly traveled away. I met a certain man, who gave me three coins with which I bought myself three loaves of bread.[29] Then, I had enough sustenance for the success of my journey. I asked the man from whom I had bought the loaves which way led directly to the river Jordan. When I knew the way, I ran along the path, weeping continually. Filled always with question upon question, I wound along the path of the day weeping.

"It had been noon when I tried to see the precious Holy Cross. When the sun was setting and nightfall drew near, I came to the church of St John the Baptist, set beside the Jordan. I went inside and prayed by myself there. Soon after, I went down to the river Jordan to wash my hands and face in the holy river. Then, I partook of the living Eucharist and the undefiled rites of our Lord Savior Christ in the same church of John, the holy forerunner and baptist. While there, I ate half of one loaf and drank from the river. I rested there for the night. Early in the morning, I traveled over the river and again began to pray to my guide St Mary, that she would direct me wherever it was her will.

"Thus, I came to this desert. From that day until this present day, I have stayed isolated, always fleeing, and waiting for my God, trusting in Him who redeems all who turn to Him from the terror of this world."

"Oh, my lady, how many years have you now lived in this desert?" Zosimus asked.

---

[29] This recalls the story of Saul, who also began his path toward redemption with three loaves of bread. See I Samuel 10:3.

"It seems to me it has been forty-seven years, since I traveled out from the holy city," the woman answered.

Zosimus said, "What could you find to eat, or on what have you fed yourself until this?"

"I brought here with me two and a half loaves of bread when I traveled across the Jordan," she answered. "In not a long time, they dried up and grew as hard as stone. I consumed those for some while."

Zosimus said to her, "Could you go through the lengths of so many seasons without caring about the passion of fleshly inclinations?"

Then, in distress, she answered, "Now you ask me about things I seriously dread! If I would remember now all the danger I underwent, and the unfortunate thoughts that often troubled me, I might suffer particular hardship again from the same thoughts."

"Oh, lady, do not leave out anything you have not told me, but reveal all the matters in order," Zosimus said.

"Abbot, believe me, for seventeen years I struggled against the gentle and unreasoning desires and lusts of beasts," she said. "When hunger would start up in me, my cravings were for the meats of flesh. I yearned for the fish that were in Egypt. I wanted the wine, which earlier I had been delighted to enjoy to drunkenness. Even now, longing for it is immense within me, because I had consumed it to excess previously when I was in the world. Also, I have had extreme thirst, because of the dearth of water here in this desert, so much so that I could hardly endure this dangerous necessity. A great yearning for shameful poems has also troubled me, when it would come into my mind to sing devilish songs I had learned earlier in the world. Weeping then, I would strike my breast with my hands, and would remind myself of my promise, and the protection I had chosen before.

"So carrying my thoughts through the desert, I arrived in front of the good image of the Holy Mother of God, who had accepted me earlier into her protection. Weeping before her, I prayed that she expel the foul thoughts from me, which tormented my pitiful soul. Overwhelmed by sorrow, I wept and harshly struck my breast. Afterward, I saw light shining all around me and a steadfast peace immediately came over me.

"Pity me now, abbot! How can I tell you my thoughts, when I fear that I might be forced to the flame of that great fire burning inside again, and my unhappy body would completely oppress me? When I would see passion rising up in such thoughts, I would prostrate myself on the earth, and saturate my cheeks with tears, because previously I had committed myself to remain on the ground until the sweet voice illuminated me, as was its custom, and expelled the distressing thoughts from me. When in need, always I have lifted up the eyes of my heart to my protector, praying to her in this desert that she would help me to true repentance, she who gave birth in purity to the Lord of all. Thus, as I said earlier, for seventeen years, I struggled against numerous dangers for all reasons until the present day. The Holy Mother of God has supported me and guided my way."

Zosimus said to her, "And did you not lack any nourishment or clothing?"

She answered him and said, "As I told you earlier, for seventeen years, I ate the loaves and then I lived on the plants I found in this desert. The clothes I had when I crossed over the Jordan were soon destroyed in the process of growing old. I endured immense hardships afterward, sometimes because of the icy coldness of winter, and sometimes because of the excessive burning of the sun's heat. I was so cruelly scorched from severe burning, and again from the severely frosty coldness of winter, that often I lay down on the earth without spirit, almost completely motionless.

"For a long time, I endured these numerous and various hardships, and wrestled with difficult temptations. Since then, until this present day, the sacred power preserved my poor soul and my body. Within myself, I have thought always about how much evil she released me from.

"Truly, I am fed with the abundant sustenance of my fulfillment, that is, with the hope of my salvation, and I am covered with the veil of God's word, He who embraces and encircles all things.[30] No one can live on bread alone,[31] but on every word that comes from the mouth of God."

When Zosimus heard her bring forth proverbs from the holy book, the Gospel, and from many others, he said to her, "Oh, mother, did you ever learn the psalms or other holy writings?"

She smiled at him when she heard this, and said, "Believe me, except for you, I have not seen any person, wild beast, or any kind of small animal, since I crossed over the river Jordan, and came here to this desert. I never learned letters nor listened to any of those who examined and read them. But, the word of God is alive, and actively teaches knowledge to people.[32]

[30] Deuteronomy 8:3.
[31] Matthew 11:44.
[32] Hebrews 4:12.

"This is the end of the things I have accomplished. I ask and implore you now, through the incarnation of God's word, to pray for me, a poor adulterer."

When she had said this, the old man ran toward her, bending his knees in order to prostrate himself on the earth. Loudly, he cried out, with sorrowful weeping, "Blessed be God, He who alone works so many miracles. And blessed be You, Lord God, who has shown me the glory which You give to those who dread You! I know as truth now that You will never abandon anyone who might seek You."[33]

She prevented the old man from continuing, and would not permit him to completely prostrate himself on the earth, saying to him, "You have heard these things, man. Further, for the sake of our Redeemer the Lord Savior Christ, I beseech you not to tell anyone about this until God liberates me from the bonds of flesh. Since these matters are now all known, travel home with peace. I will be shown to you at this same time a year from now. You will see me truly. However, do now as I ask you. When your holy fast of Lent arrives next year, do not journey across the Jordan from your monastery as usual."

Again, Zosimus marveled that she knew the rule of the monastery so precisely, but he said nothing else, except that he would glorify God, who gives so much to people who love Him when they ask in their prayers.

"As I said before, Zosimus," she said again, "remain in your monastery, because even though you might want to travel here, you will not be able to. On the evening of the holy festival, which is the Holy Thursday before the Lord's Easter day, put a portion of the sacred body and the life-giving blood into a hallowed cup and bring it with you. But, wait for me on the side of the Jordan that belongs to the world until I come to you. Since I partook of the life-giving mystery of the Lord's body and His blood in the church of the blessed forerunner before I traveled across the Jordan, I have not enjoyed nor tasted the sacred sustenance. Therefore, I beg you not to refuse my request, that you bring me the sacred and life-giving mysteries of the Eucharist at the time when the Savior shared the sacred meal with His companions. Also, tell John, abbot of the monastery where you are, that he should think sincerely about himself and his flock, because there are some customs which should be corrected and improved. But, don't tell him about these things until God commands you."

[33] Psalms 9:10.

Having said this, she asked the old man for a prayer, and hurried quickly to the inner desert.

Then, Zosimus prostrated himself on the floor, kissing the place where her feet had stood, praising God. Giving great thanks, he turned back. By the same path of the desert on which he had come there before, he returned, praising and blessing our Lord Savior Christ. At the same time they came for Easter customs, he traveled to the monastery.

All that year, he diligently concealed the vision, not daring to say anything about even the least matter he had seen. To himself, he always prayed earnestly that God would again reveal to him that longed-for face. With countless sighs, he waited through the slowness of the year's course.

Then, when the time of the fast of Holy Lent arrived, the Lord's day which we call the Holy Day, the brothers traveled out as usual after the prayers and psalm-singing. He was left by himself in the monastery, very eagerly staying there because of a weakness of the body, and because Zosimus remembered the holy command she had given to him, that even though he might want to travel out from his monastery he would not be able to.

Not many days later, he recovered from his sickness, and served in the monastery. When the monks returned home, and assembled together on the evening of the holy feast day, he did as he was asked earlier, and placed a portion of the undefiled body and precious blood of our Lord Savior Christ into one little chalice. In his hands, he carried a small basket, filled with dried figs, the fruit of palm trees, which we call dates, and a few lentils soaked in water.

In the evening, he arrived at the shore of the river Jordan, and waited sorrowfully there for the holy woman's arrival. Zosimus did not sleep at all. Intently, he watched the desert, and deliberated about it, and said to himself, "What if she has already come here, and did not notice me, and then turned and left?"

After saying this, he wept bitterly. He raised his eyes to the heavens and prayed humbly to God, saying thus, "Do not separate me, Lord, from the sight which you first revealed to me, so that I might not turn from here in vain, bearing reproach for my sins."

While he prayed in tears, another thought occurred to him. He said, "And if she comes, how will she travel over these waters, since there is no ship here in which she might come to unworthy me? Oh unhappy me, that such a sharp insight isolates me!"

As he thought this, he saw where she stood on the other side of the river. Upon seeing her, Zosimus rose up joyfully, with immense gladness, and praised God. But, his mind doubted how she could travel over the river Jordan. Then, he saw that she blessed the river Jordan with the sign of Christ's cross. As soon as she dipped the sign of the cross into the river, the brightness of the moon illuminated all the darkness of the night. Thus, she went upon the wavering waves, coming toward him, as if on dry land.

Zosimus marveled. When he tried to kneel to her, she called out from the river, trying to prevent him.

"What are you doing, abbot?" she said. "You know that you are a priest of God, and have the sacred mysteries with you!"

Immediately obeying her, he rose up. As soon as she came off the river, she said, "Father, bless me."

A great amazement came over him at such a glorious spectacle, and he said, "Oh you trustworthy woman, God has promised you earlier that those who have purified themselves will be like Him. Glory be to You, Lord God, who has shown me, through this hand-maid of Yours, how much my own perfection should be measured against that of others."

After he had said this, Mary asked that he begin the prayer of belief, that is the Creed of God, and afterward the Lord's Prayer, the Pater Noster. When these had been completed, she gave the old man a kiss of peace, as is customary, and took the holy mysteries of Christ's body and blood with outstretched hands. Looking up to Heaven, grieving with tears, she said, "Lord, allow your handmaid to go in peace, according to your word, because my eyes have seen your salvation."[34]

"Have mercy on me, abbot," she said again to the old man. "Now fulfill the other request of my prayer. Go straight to your monastery with the peace of God, and in about a year's time come again to the stream you know where we two first spoke. I beg you, for God's sake, not to hold back from this. When you arrive, you will see me, as God wills."

"Oh, that I would be allowed to follow your footsteps and enjoy the sight of your precious face!" he said then. "But, mother, I ask that you grant me, an old man, this one little request; that you would agree to accept what I have brought here. Take this basket that I have brought."

With her fingertips, she touched the lentils, which are peas, and put the amount of three grains in her mouth. She said that this gift was sufficient for one who wanted to keep her soul secure and

[34] Luke 2:29.

unstained. To the aged man, she said, "Pray for me, and protect my misfortune."

In tears, he beseeched her to pray with the assembly of Holy God and he touched her feet. But, she left him then. Weeping and grieving, he did not dare to hinder her in any way for he was unable to hinder her in anything. She began again to touch the Jordan with the sign of the Holy Cross, and went away over the wavering waves of the river, as she had done earlier.

As Zosimus returned with great rejoicing, suddenly he became filled with great awe, sorrowfully reproaching himself that he should have asked the name of the holy woman. Even so, he hoped he might learn it the following year.

Once he had gone through the year's course, he came into the broad desert and hurried eagerly toward that glorious sight. For a long time, he traveled there, seeking here and there to discern any clear sign of the shrine of his longed-for vision and desire. With keen eyes, he intently gazed to both the right and the left, as if he were a skillful hunter who wanted to catch that sweetest beast.

When he could not find anything moving, he grew overwhelmed with tears. With uplifted eyes, he asked, "Show me, Lord, that hidden gold-hoard which you earlier deemed me worthy to behold. For Your glory, I pray to You, Lord."

After he had prayed, he came to the place marked by the stream where they had first spoken, and saw there on the other side, shining as if it were the sun, the body of this holy woman, lying lifelessly. Her hands were placed, as was the custom, and she was turned eastward.

He ran there at once, and washed her feet with his tears. Truly, he did not presume to touch any other part of the body. Weeping greatly, he performed a prayer for her burial with psalm-singing and other prayers related to such matters. Then, he began to think about whether this would have pleased her. While he thought about this, some writing appeared inscribed on the earth there, recording this, "Abbot Zosimus, bury and show compassion to the body of Mary. Give to the earth what is hers, and the dust to the dust. Also, add that in the world you pray for me, who have departed on the ninth night of the month which is April, that is the Ides of April, on the Lord's feast day, and after partaking of the Eucharist."

When the old man had read the letters, he first sought how they had been written, because she herself had said earlier that she never learned any of what he saw. Still, he rejoiced much to know her name and to understand clearly that, as soon as she had received the sacred mysteries the time before at the Jordan, she had come there and immediately had departed from the world. The path that Zosimus had traversed with much effort in twenty days, Mary had accomplished completely in the course of one hour and at once had departed to the Lord.

After Zosimus had glorified God and saturated his own body with tears, he said, "Now it is time, poor Zosimus, that you accomplish what has been asked of you. But, unfortunate person, what am I now to do? I don't know with what I might dig, since I am lacking both a spade and a mattock."

As he spoke silently in his mind, he saw a small part of a tree lying there. Very eagerly, he began to dig with it, but the earth was so hard that it could not be hollowed out, since he was so weakened from fasting and the long work, and was burdened by panting and sweat. Heavily from the depths of his heart, he lamented.

When he looked around him, he saw an exceedingly large lion standing by the holy body, and it licked the footprints. He was frightened with terror by this huge wild beast, especially because earlier the holy woman had told him that she had never seen any wild beasts there. So, immediately, he warded himself on all sides with the sign of the cross, and with the power of she who lay there. At this, the lion started to fawn at the old man, and greeted him by moving his limbs.

"Oh you, most huge, wild beast," Zosimus said to the lion, "if you were sent here from God so that you might entrust this body of God's holy handmaid to the earth, fulfill the labor of your service now. I am so weakened by old age that I cannot dig, nor have I anything appropriate with which to perform this work, nor can I hurry on such a great path to bring such here. But you, by sacred decree, might now achieve this work with your claws, until we two have committed this holy body to the earth."

Immediately after his words, the lion worked with its claws to scrape a hole with its forelegs as large as necessary to bury the saint. Pouring forth a multitude of prayers, Zosimus washed her feet with his tears, and prayed that she intercede for them all. Thus, he covered the body with earth, as naked as when he had first met her, except for the protection of a torn piece of the garment Zosimus had thrown to her earlier, that Mary had wrapped around a certain part of her body. Together they turned, the lion departing into the inner desert, as though the mildest lamb, and Zosimus departing to his monastery, glorifying, blessing, and honoring God with praise.

As soon as he came to the monastery, he recounted everything to them from the beginning. He concealed nothing he had seen or heard about the matters in order for them all to worship the glory of God.

With awe and love and great faith, they celebrated the day of her blessed departure.

Afterward, as the saint had foretold earlier, John recognized how to improve some of the monastic customs. With God's support, he corrected them at once.

Zosimus served the monastery for a hundred years, and then departed to the Lord. Let it be glory for our Lord Savior Christ, who lives and rules always and forever.[35] AMEN.

---

[35] Literally translated as something like "always in the world of all worlds," the Old English term *ealra worulda woruld ealra* is commonly translated in the sense of *forever and ever*, as in the phrase, *per omnia secula saeculorum*, commonly used in Latin liturgical texts. This same phrase also concludes the *Life of St Eugenia*.

Interpretive Essay

The Gendered Body as Spiritual Problem and Spiritual Answer in the Lives of Women Saints

The female body in the Middle Ages was not so much a source of controversy and discussion as it was of pain, fear, and frustration for men as well as women. Women were perceived as the bearers of carnal temptation; their bodies, physical reminders of original sin. For medieval culture, the impulses of physical passion and sexuality were part of humanity's punishment for Eve's original temptation of Adam in the Garden of Eden. As Eve was responsible for humanity's fall from grace, so too, as Eve's physical and spiritual heirs, medieval women had the latent potential to cause spiritual and social destruction. These daughters of Eve were considered dangerous to society because of the passions their bodies evoked in men. The medieval church understood such passions to be antithetical to both reason and faith. New Testament scripture and the writings of the Church Fathers insisted that physical and carnal pleasures distracted the individual's attention from its most important goal, the contemplation of God. While both men and women were directed to control their desires for such pleasure, theological doctrine emphasized that a woman's physical body, her female identity, provided the vehicle through which the destructive forces of sexuality were channeled into society. As a result, it was largely the responsibility of women to deny and repress the desires of the body. To counter the female body's potential for social and spiritual harm, church authorities recommended virginity as the primary means by which women could "transcend the weakness and limitations inherent in their gender."[1]

Although an impossible goal for many, the state of total virginity was considered the highest achievement for a medieval Christian woman.[2] Women were taught that to achieve their highest spiritual

---

[1] Jane Tibbetts Schulenburg, *Forgetful of their Sex: Female Sanctity and Society, ca 500–1100* (Chicago: University of Chicago Press, 1998), p. 128.

[2] Much scholarship has treated the subject of virginity in the Middle Ages more extensively than the scope of this essay permits. Some of the works most useful

aspirations they must transform their female biology by practicing virginity, and thereby become genderless in God. Scriptural testimony in support of efforts to transcend gender was found in Paul's statement that "there is neither male nor female; for you are all one in Christ Jesus."[3] Matched against the destructive forces residing within the female body, the virtuous power of virginity provided an instrument through which women could achieve spiritual transformation and redemption. Yet, while virginity carried an immense power for salvation, a daily, heroic battle was necessary to maintain it in a world that devalued women's bodies and in which rape was common. Saints' lives, like those translated here, provided models for such heroic, virginal defense. As Jane Tibbetts Schulenburg describes, lives like those of Agatha, Agnes and Cecilia, served "to underscore the reality that virginity entailed inordinate struggle, vigorous, aggressive defense, but also, ultimately, great rewards."[4]

But, religious advocation of virginity introduced practical difficulties for the church as well as for individual women. Economic and political realities required them to marry, bear children, and manage households. New Christians had to be born from women's bodies in order for Christianity to continue in the world. As a result, the patriarchal institutions of medieval Christian Europe uncomfortably tried to reconcile the practical necessity of the reproductive aspects of the female body with the religious requirement that it be rejected. Negotiating the gendered female body remained profoundly problematic for both the medieval church and for women themselves. Although

for considering the texts translated in this collection are: Clarissa W. Atkinson, ed., *Immaculate and Powerful: The Female in Sacred Image and Social Reality* (Boston: Beacon Press, 1985); Peter Brown, *The Body and Society: Men, Women, and Sexual Renunciation in Early Christianity* (New York: Columbia Press, 1988); Lynda L. Coon, *Sacred Fictions: Holy Women and Hagiography in Late Antiquity* (Philadelphia: University of Philadelphia Press, 1997); Thomas J. Heffernan, *Sacred Biography: Saints and their Biographers in the Middle Ages* (London: Oxford University Press, 1988); Jo Ann McNamara, "Sexual Equality and the Cult of Virginity" in *Women in Early Christianity*, ed. David M. Scholer, Studies in Early Christianity: A Collection of Scholarly Essays, ed. Everett Ferguson (New York: Garland, 1993), pp. 219–33; Barbara Newman, *From Virile Woman to WomanChrist,* Studies in Medieval Religion and Literature (Philadelphia: University of Pennsylvania Press, 1995); Joyce Salisbury, *Church Fathers, Independent Virgins* (London: Verso, 1991); and Jane Tibbetts Schulenburg, *Forgetful of their Sex: Female Sanctity and Society, ca 500–1100* (Chicago: University of Chicago Press, 1998).

[3]   Galatians 3:28.
[4]   Jane Tibbetts Schulenburg, *Forgetful of their Sex*, p. 135.

they were encouraged to lead lives of chastity and conduct themselves always as devout citizens of the faith, the enlightened, genderless state suggested by Paul was an impossible fantasy for most medieval women. Any serious contemplation of women transforming themselves into sexless, genderless beings, whose bodies reflected only the purest spiritual constructs, was not only unrealistic, but culturally subversive. Because such an insistence on celibacy involved a woman's denial of her own sexuality, some contemporary scholars have argued that it is "but one more attestation of the patriarchal and misogynist oppression in the early church."[5] However, another position, summarized by David M. Scholer, maintains that "this aspect of life for women should be understood in its own cultural context as 'liberation' and empowerment for women, even though it is surrounded by various oppressive patriarchal features."[6] How then, within such a cultural context and surrounded by such forces, could women of the Middle Ages both control their own lives and enhance their spiritual development without jeopardizing their personal and political identities?

To answer such problems, women saints' lives provided medieval women with approved sources for spiritual reflection. By inviting medieval women to reflect on the relationship between their bodies and souls, such texts portray women controlling their lives and bodies in ways that were religiously sanctioned. The stories of saints, such as Æthelthryth, Agatha, Agnes, Cecilia, Eugenia, Euphrosyne, Lucy, and Mary of Egypt, illustrated the varieties of pride and strength with which women addressed social and spiritual conflicts arising from the inherent tension between biological gender and Christian philosophy. Clare Lees explains this conflict when she writes, "Female saints confront and overcome the deadliness of their bodies and the deadliness of their sexuality time and again."[7] By appropriating the same ideal of virginity that was intended to limit women's bodies and autonomy, these women saints take control of their bodies by transforming their sexuality. In so doing, they establish authority over the direction of their lives and, especially, of their souls. Just as today's feminists assert the right of contemporary

---

5   David M. Scholer, ed., "Introduction" in *Women in Early Christianity*, Studies in Early Christianity: A Collection of Scholarly Essays, ed. Everett Ferguson (New York: Garland, 1993), p. xii.

6   Scholer, p. xiii.

7   Clare A. Lees, "Engendering Religious Desire: Sex, Knowledge, and Christian Identity in Anglo-Saxon England," *Journal of Medieval and Early Modern Studies* 27:1 (Winter 1997): 16–45, p. 32.

women to control their own bodies and lives, women saints' lives invited medieval women to regain control of their bodies and, consequently, their lives, without sacrificing spiritual goals or social positions. Thus, women saints' lives serve as early reflections of the insights learned by our own women's movement which affirm that, "as women, we cannot determine the direction of our lives as long as others control our bodies."[8]

Such models provided ordinary medieval women[9] not so much with patterns on which to base their lives, but with encouragement for their efforts to negotiate day-to-day struggles between their faith and their physical forms. Influential religious women like the Saxon canoness Hrotsvitha even wrote works of their own in order to "stress the importance of virginity as an active choice, as a vocation, and as an emblem of spiritual leadership," for both the saints themselves and for the women of the time.[10] By contemplating the efforts of ancient women to maintain their intellectual and spiritual integrity when confronted with attitudes that brought disrespect to their bodies, medieval women found support for their own lives. Yet, the kind of support these texts may have provided medieval and later women may not always have been intended by the primarily male writers, disseminators, and advocates of such texts. Even though the intentions of church authorities in producing women saints' lives were to provide restrictive models, they "could be 'read' in a variety of ways by their female audiences."[11] It is clear that women in monastic communities as well as secular settings interpreted such texts as offering positive options for incorporating spiritual achievement with the control of physicality. The extreme behavior described in many women saints' lives, however, would have been ordinarily viewed in medieval culture

as transgressing the boundaries of permissible diversity.

Thus in some cases the "alternative reading" or adaptation of

---

8   Bernadette J. Brooten, "Paul's Views on the Nature of Women and Female Homoeroticism" in *Immaculate and Powerful: The Female in Sacred Image and Social Reality*, ed. Clarissa W. Atkinson (Boston: Beacon Press, 1985), p. 62.

9   I do not mean to suggest here that women saints' lives served devotional purposes for women only. As I have discussed in the Introduction to this collection, women saints' lives held great interest for both men and women. However, since this essay explores the impact of holy legends on medieval women, I will focus my discussion here exclusively on the female audiences of these texts.

10   Elizabeth Alvilda Petroff, *Body and Soul: Essays on Medieval Women and Mysticism* (Oxford: Oxford University Press, 1994), p. 84.

11   Jane Tibbetts Schulenburg, *Forgetful of their Sex*, p. 407.

saints' extraordinary behavior to one's own special circumstances was not at all that which had been originally intended
by the male redactors. These saints' Lives could then be
appropriated by women for their own purposes and refash-
ioned as positive models or vehicles for empowerment.[12]

Nevertheless, regardless of their original intentions or their
explicit theological purposes and regardless of the fact that these
texts may or may not reflect the actual experiences of historical
women, women saints' lives establish a consistency of female cultural experience that resonates with the experiences of women at the
turn of the second millennium, no less than with their original audience at the turn of the first millennium.

Much like contemporary women, medieval women struggled to
maintain control of their female identity within cultures that perceived the female body as an object for violence and abuse as well as
a temptation toward physical excitement and sexual pleasure. In
modern media and advertising, the female body is manipulated to
control the desires of the populace. Although different in intention,
such manipulation parallels the efforts of religious authorities who
sought control over female sexuality and, thereby, sought to influence the development and needs of medieval culture. However, even
in the effort to portray religious control of female bodies, many
women saints' lives establish the equally important need for women
to have autonomy over their own bodies. As religion gains control
over female sexual identity by placing women in religiously-
motivated circumstances, so too women saints' lives portray women
who acquire control of their physicality by turning faith into a
weapon for their bodies' defense. This is especially true in the stories
of the virgin saints who are young women.

In such texts, sexuality is understood to be the primary expression
of the female body's weakness or its "frailty." Control of the
woman's sexual experience incites the struggle between good and
evil, between God and the Devil-linked pagans. Asserting authority
over the sexual intentions others wish to impose on her body
becomes the young virgin saint's path to confirming her personal
power as well as God's ultimate victory. Take the story of Agnes, the
youngest saint in this collection, as an example. Described as thirteen
at the time of her martyrdom, Agnes' piety is remarkable for her
youth. But precisely what is extraordinary about Agnes' devotion? It

[12] Jane Tibbetts Schulenburg, *Forgetful of their Sex*, p. 408.

is her emphatic insistence that Christ has already made her His bride. Agnes publicly defends her rejection of the attentions of the un-named son of the prefect Simpronius by describing the romantic and erotically suggestive nature of her relationship with Christ. In eloquent speeches evocative of the Song of Songs, Agnes tells how she has "another lover, more noble than you" (47) to whom she is betrothed. Agnes tells how Christ chose the young virgin as His bride by giving her "His ring of faith" (47), encircling her "right hand . . . with shining gems" (47), adorning her with "inconceivable honors" (47), dressing her in "a robe woven of gold" (47), and most significantly by putting "His mark upon [her] face" (47). But the choice of Agnes as His spouse is not only His; she reciprocates by willingly choosing Him. She confirms this choice when she says, "With all devotion, I will always keep my promise to the one to whom I have committed myself" (47), and later reiterates with "I cannot insult Him by choosing another, and I will not abandon Him, who has betrothed me with love" (47). She articulates her choice of the love offered in this spiritual marriage over a secular marriage to Simpronius' son by stating "I rejected your son, who is truly a man, and I cannot by any means look on his face because of the love of my Christ" (48). For Agnes, Christ is the idealized suitor, lover, and husband. He nourishes her with marvelous food ("milk and honey" (47)) and His body attracts her ("His appearance is more beautiful, and His love more delightful") (47). Reflecting the *sponsa Christi*, spouse of Christ, motif[13] common in hagiographic texts with women subjects, their marital interactions are patterned on secular relationships and are explicitly physical. They have a "bridal bed" (47) which is prepared for her "with delights" (47); "His pure arms" (47) embrace her, and "His fair body is united" (47) with Agnes' body. His touch is intensely fulfilling to her, and she actively partici-pates in their union. In fact, she portrays herself as the initiator by using the first person as an active agent when she asserts, "When I love Him, I am completely pure. When I touch Him, I am unstained. When I submit to Him, I am still a maiden" (47). In addition, their physical interaction implies not only superior sexual satisfaction for Agnes, but it also engenders spiritual offspring that perfect her womanhood without restricting it for "children will not fail in this

---

[13] Hugh Magennis discusses this theme in detail in his article of specific relevance to our subject, "Occurrence of Nuptial Imagery in Old English Hagiographical Texts," *English Language Notes* 33.4 (June 1996): 1–9.

marriage, where there is conception without pain, and continual fertility" (47).

Yet, regardless of the religious context of these romantic, sexually charged speeches, it is the saint's adamance about choosing her bridegroom and the nature of this experience that has particular relevance to this discussion. Although only thirteen, Agnes presents herself as a completely fulfilled woman. She has the ideal husband, who is perfectly romantic and allows her unrestricted access to satisfying her physical needs. By choosing Him, she maintains control of her virginal body. In fact, with her choice, Agnes makes it possible for her body to become consummately female, in that she preserves her physical virginity from the defilement of actual intercourse and exists in a spiritual state in which she conceives in constant fecundity. Her insistence on the reciprocity of their idyllic model of love suggests a marriage based on emotional egalitarianism. In this way, Agnes' refusal to consent to secular marriage with the son of Simpronius frees her to express her feminine identity through the ultimate marriage and empowers her body to experience all the possibilities of female expression without restriction.

However, in addition to the descriptions of her spiritual marriage to Christ, this saint's life provides other proof of the power authorized by the female body. Her rejection of his son motivates Simpronius to command that Agnes not only be taken to a house of prostitution, but that she be led there naked. Stripping her clothes is an act by which Simpronius seeks to make Agnes' naked body public property. In addition, by compelling her to be taken to a house of prostitution, he seeks to deny her control of her own body and to appropriate her sexuality to serve the will of others. But, her trust in God causes her hair to grow, enveloping her completely as soon as her clothes are removed from her body. With its ancient association with female beauty and fertility, Agnes' hair shields her body from sight and, thereby, preserves it from public contamination. Acting as her shield, the beauty and fertility residing in her youthful body are Agnes' alone; it is her trust in God and her bridegroom Christ that grants her the ability to command her own body. Not only can her trust in God allow her to control who sees her physical body in public, but, once she enters the house of the prostitutes, an angel of God illuminates the house with such a bright light that it dazzles the sight of those within, preventing further disclosure of her femininity. Her faith gives the saint further protection in the form of a shining tunic, which proves God's attention and inhibits any assaults on her sexuality. When Simpronius' son tries to enter the house with the intention of forcibly enjoying the sexual potential of her body, this young woman's faith again gives her physical control, and he is killed instantly. Significantly, he is killed not by the angel of God, but "by the Devil, whom he foolishly obeyed" (50). The son's shameful lust for Agnes is foolish, because it is inspired by evil, and it enslaves him. He allows it to take over his will. Agnes' will, on the other hand, is hers to control and, by directing it toward a proper faith in God, she is able to defend her own body. Within its shield of hair and the shining tunic, Agnes' body radiates a power wholly female and completely protected. By joining her body in marriage to Christ and choosing to trust in God, Agnes takes charge of her body and her life. While some modern readers might find the story of her subsequent death tragic, the text demands that we view Agnes as a young woman of power and strength, who employs her religious faith to retain control of her female identity manifested in her body, to own the expression of her womanly sexuality, and to authorize her marital choices.

Agnes is not alone in this group of saints whose faith in God provides her with a foundation from which to exercise the power of her own will. Agatha also affirms the power of her gendered body to enhance the glory of God. Like Agnes, Agatha rejects a pagan suitor, who is the slave of the Devil and ruled by his own lustfulness. Enraged by Agatha's refusal of him, Quintianus, like Simpronius, orders the maiden to be delivered to a prostitute. With her nine "shameless daughters" (38), the prostitute Aphrodisia is expected to teach Agatha the ways of prostitution and force her mind to be "perverted by the seductions of the prostitutes" (38). Again, we see the theme of an attempt to take away forcibly the woman saint's control of her sexuality and make it available for public use. Although "sometimes alluring, sometimes terrifying" (38), Aphrodisia and her daughters clearly employ the sexuality of their bodies to turn Agatha's mind to carnal desires. Despite them, the saint's will holds firm. Defiantly, she counters their efforts: "Your words are like the wind, but they cannot uproot my steadfast thought which is firmly grounded" (38). Using such nature imagery, Agatha contrasts the instability of their physicality put into public service with the permanence of her ability to resist sexual temptation by serving only God. Aphrodisia recognizes her own powerlessness against the strength of a will supported by such faith. As the text notes, "When Aphrodisia saw that she could not bend the mind of the maiden with her shameful temptations, she went to Quintianus and said thus to him, 'Stones may soften . . . before the faith can ever be extinguished from Agatha's breast' " (38).

Agatha's female body continues to provide a means by which the saint operates control over those who would hinder her will. Quintianus commands that her body be twisted on the rack "like a rope" (40), but then focuses his torture on that most female part of the saint's physical body, her breasts. After her breasts have been twisted in the rack, he has one of them cut off in an attempt to acquire control of her feminine sexuality by removing its representative from her body. Her response denies the sexual implications of this act and shifts the meaning of the mutilation to the qualities of nurturing motherhood inherent in the womanly form. Although viciously injured, Agatha turns his victory to shame by saying, "Does it not shame you to cut off that which you yourself would suck?" (41). As he twisted her body on the rack, so the exertion of her will not only twists his gratification, but it also preserves the wholeness of her femininity transformed in her soul. Using nourishment as a metaphor for this transformative act of faith, Agatha insists "I have my breast sound in my soul, because I am completely fed by my senses" (41). The power of such transcendence, inspired by Agatha's own personal will, is lost on Quintianus, even after her devotion motivates God to restore her breast as physical proof of the spiritual truth of her words.

Recalling the efforts of Simpronius to destroy Agnes' autonomy by making her naked body a spectacle for public regard, Quintianus further attempts to appropriate Agatha's power by mastering her sexuality when he commands that she be rolled naked across a floor covered with burning embers and shards of tiles. Where before he had tried to remove the expression of her sexual control by removing her breast, with this torture Quintianus seeks to invade its perfection by puncturing and burning holes in her skin. Yet, still the female body cannot be mastered. Taking its power from God's authority, Agatha's will again denies Quintianus his victory. Before his order can be executed, an earthquake prevents this additional mutilation of Agatha's body. While the text never explicitly indicates that Agatha commanded the power to cause the earthquake, the reader must surely be expected to recall her earlier words to Aphrodisia in which she associated the will that controlled her body with the firmness of the ground. The shaking of the earth that suspends her torture is divinely controlled, but it also mirrors her desire to protect her naked body, the embodiment of her womanly will, from further physical damage. As Agatha previously had used the earth as a metaphor for her own ability to withstand carnal temptation, so the earth itself acknowledges its affinity to her by providing Agatha the means to keep the surface of her body, her skin, as intact as her faith, an external intactness that reflects an internal physical and spiritual wholeness. Agatha's insistence on sexual virginity mirrors the preservation of her spiritual virtue. Her sanctity arises from a collaboration between the female body and the individual will, together choosing to wield their authority in honor of God.

Cecilia is another young woman saint whose strength of purpose keeps her sexuality under her own control and directs others to a virtuous attention on God. Although the beginning of her life relates how she continually exhibited extreme devotion to her Christian faith, her family arranged for her to be married to a nobleman named Valerian, who was not a Christian. But it was the requirement that she give up her virginity, rather than Valerian's lack of faith, that caused Cecilia grief over the impending marriage. As with Agnes and Agatha, it is crucial to Cecilia's identity as a Christian woman that she be "shielded from any defilement or intercourse with a man, . . . so that she might be allowed to serve Christ in purity" (58). By denying her the authority to determine how best to use her body for the enrichment of her faith, the marriage would force her to grant sexual control of her body to her husband. Cecilia's legend tells how she, prior to her wedding, exerted the dominance of her will over her body's needs by clothing herself in haircloth and by fasting. Yet, despite such physical exertions and her prayers, Cecilia's wedding takes place against her will. The secular world's desire to subjugate her female body to its intentions prevails.

On her wedding night, instead of continuing her attempts to negate her sexuality, Cecilia employs its power over her husband in her bridal bed. The text is not explicit here; yet the subtext of this scene cannot be ignored. She is a young woman, a virgin, lying in bed next to a man for the first time in her life. Undoubtedly, he is preparing to consummate their marriage. The songs she had sung at her bridal feast about keeping her body undefiled have had no impact on her husband. It is his marital right to make her body his through sexual intercourse. Her female sexuality should become his charge. But, it is at this moment that Cecilia, a "wise maiden" (58), turns to him and begins his education, telling him about an angel of God who protects her and will kill him if he has sex with her. The reader must, of course, imagine that Valerian was taken aback at his new wife's words. In addition, the text makes it plain that her words have frightened him. Trying to regain the autonomy over her physical body that her words have supplanted, Valerian replies, "If another retainer is more intimate with you than I, then I will kill him and you together with him" (59). Here, the implication is that, if Cecilia has granted sexual control of her body to another man, Valerian's status as her husband gives him complete control over her very life. But, again, Cecilia uses the power of words to take back control of her own life and body. Unconcernedly, Cecilia begins to teach Valerian about Christianity. That Valerian listens to her is a testament to the strength of her will as well as to the truth of her faith. Nevertheless, Cecilia's beautiful young body[14] lying next to him certainly has its own persuasive impact on his willingness to consider what she has to say. With surprisingly little effort, Cecilia not only converts him to Christianity, but also convinces him that they should both remain celibate in their marriage in order to achieve their highest spiritual potential. In this way, Cecilia's gendered body, lying controlled and chaste in her own marriage bed, becomes an instrument that allows her will to function at its greatest spiritual capacity. The heightened sexual attractiveness endowed by her beauty, youth, and virginal status, together with her verbal eloquence, affords Cecilia the power to control her own destiny and her devotion to God. It is specifically because her body is female that she achieves salvation. Elizabeth Alvilda Petroff articulates the characteristics of this virginal power, although her discussion concerns Agnes, when she writes,

> Virginity has three outstanding qualities: it is beautiful; it is heroic or victorious; and it is eloquent. The beauty of virginity and of these virgins attracts others, whom it has a compelling power to transform. The active choice of a virgin's life brings about an inner transformation, resulting in extraordinary strength, perseverance, and eloquence.[15]

Like Cecilia, Euphrosyne also wants to avoid marriage in order to preserve the spiritual virtue she gains by remaining physically virginal. However, although he is a devout Christian and Euphrosyne's birth was the result of holy prayers to God, her father, Paphnuntius, avoids consideration of her wishes in favor of marrying her to a wealthy man so that he might increase his own wealth. As she tells the monk who visits her father's household, "My father wants to give me to a man, but I do not want myself to be tainted" (83). While

---

14 Although Cecilia's beauty has not been described at this point in the text, the importance of her beauty, nobility, wisdom, and youth is highlighted later in the text.

15 Elizabeth Alvilda Petroff, *Body and Soul: Essays on Medieval Women and Mysticism*, (Oxford: Oxford University Press, 1994), p. 85.

Euphrosyne's father views her female body as a financial asset[16] rightfully under his control, Euphrosyne accepts the monk's assertion that she must "conquer the temptations of the flesh" (83) in order to achieve her soul's salvation. Knowing that the sexual component of marriage would deny her the ability to redeem her soul through the practice of virginity, Euphrosyne seeks a practical answer to the spiritual barrier imposed by her identity as a woman.

The answer she finds is no less shocking than Agnes' answer of her marriage to Christ. But, Euphrosyne's approach to the problem of her female body is completely opposite that of Agnes. Instead of insisting that her womanhood be both erotically and spiritually fulfilled by divine marriage, Euphrosyne controls her feminine identity by rejecting her body altogether. To do so, she disguises herself as a young male eunuch and joins a male monastery. She does so to avoid discovery, reasoning that, "If I journeyed now to a monastery for women, my father would seek me there. Then, he would take me by force for my bridegroom's sake. But I will journey to a monastery for men where no one would expect me" (84). Although for modern readers Euphrosyne's deception rather than her physical body is spiritually problematic, the text is never concerned with her deceit.

The tension between Euphrosyne's female identity and her spiritual aspirations continues throughout this story. Even disguised she "was so beautiful in appearance" (85) that the other monks were tempted by her "fairness" (85). Regardless of the homosexual implications here, the inner truth, to which the reader is privy, is that, within medieval culture, it is the nature of Euphrosyne's female body to encourage sexual temptation. Because it is so difficult for the monks to control their desires in her presence, the abbot of the monastery isolates her from the larger community by bidding her to remain in her cell. Yet, Euphrosyne does not simply accept this control of her body. Instead, she takes specific actions of her own to further suppress the threat innate to her female physicality. Of her own will, she controls the state of her body with excessive devotional practices. While her impersonation of a sexless eunuch granted her some protection from the dangers of her womanhood, her renunciation of her body's needs completes her transformation from a female to something other. This transformation also provides her with the means to effect change in her relationship with her father, who comes

---

[16] When he discovers his daughter is missing, Paphnuntius states that Euphrosyne is the "comfort" of his life, and that he also associates her loss with being deprived of riches and having his possessions destroyed.

to her for spiritual counsel, believing her to be a eunuch. As a mar-
riageable woman, Euphrosyne's body was a currency to be spent as
her father saw fit, but as a eunuch, Euphrosyne's will controls the
distribution of spiritual knowledge to her father. Euphosyne's denial
of her female body has paradoxically established the authority of her
will. Such an assertion of her will is reflected in Euphrosyne's statement on her death-bed that it was her lifelong desire that she "be
allowed to end the course of [her] life as a man."

Although Euphrosyne insists that God is responsible for fulfilling
this desire, the reader cannot help but recall the sheer fortitude of her
own will which allowed to go beyond controlling the nature of her
feminine physique and accomplish her own spiritual transformation.
Her choices to avoid marriage, to disguise herself as a eunuch, to join
a male monastery, to restrict severely the natural functions of her
body through religious observances, all concealing her biological
and familial identity in order to become her father's spiritual teacher,
demonstrate Euphrosyne's personal power. Nevertheless, it is her
very nature as a woman that compels her to such extremity of devotion. In the end, it is this same female body that reasserts itself and
demands recognition not only for the accomplishments it has
inspired, but also for its latent power. As Clare Lees describes the
revelation of Euphrosyne's gender after her death, the now undis-
guised female body of the saint, "her flesh on view against her will,"
is not "a sign of fallen humanity, but of the redeemed, sexed body."[17]
When a blind monk kisses the saint's corpse and regains his sight, it
is not only God who "worked such miracles in the womanly and delicate form" (89), but also the determination of Euphrosyne herself.

While the stories of all four remaining saints in this collection
could provide similar evidence for women's ability to use their wills
to exert control over their gendered biologies, the examples of
Agnes, Agatha, Cecilia, and Euphrosyne establish a useful spectrum
of possibilities through which to consider the relationship between
sanctity and individual autonomy. The lives of these women establish compelling ancient perspectives on themes important to contemporary audiences: (1) that women's bodies can be powerful forces for
effecting social and spiritual change; (2) that women have the right
of control over bodies; and (3) that female identity is the result of the
union of body, mind and spirit. Literary though their stance might be,

---

[17] Clare A. Lees, "Engendering Religious Desire: Sex, Knowledge, and Christian
Identity in Anglo-Saxon England," *Journal of Medieval and Early Modern
Studies* 27:1 (Winter 1997): 35.

the heroic struggles of such women saints to lead autonomous lives of purpose parallel the efforts of young women today. For medieval women, the legends reflect their endeavors to negotiate a balance between carnality and chastity, the sacred and the secular, the desires of the individual and the good of the community. Complementing the continental development of such texts, the culture of Anglo-Saxon England that produced these particular texts maintained a long heritage of Germanic heroism that included chaste, strong-willed women.[18] Such traditions, accentuated in these Old English adaptations of Latin texts, would not have been lost on the women in their audience, no matter how carefully religious authorities insisted these narratives glorified only God. The *Beowulf* poet's assertion that his hero's success depends on "God's wisdom, fate, and the mind of man"[19] must be recast only slightly to fit the pattern of these saintly heroes. The victories of these women rest on the power of their bodies, the will they direct to God, and the faith to control their own destiny. Using heroic conventions clothed in feminine garb, such saints' lives address the spiritual problem of how medieval women could achieve religious fulfillment when weighed down by the carnality considered central to female experience. The answer rests in the female body itself. It is the woman saint's gendered sexuality that makes the spiritual difference. As described by one recent scholar, "These saints, seemingly represented as non-sexual, not-women, even not human, in fact remain female, sexed, and human, especially at moments of transcendence."[20] Radical, subversive, and transgressive as the lives of these women might seem within the culture of tenth-century England as well as within their original cultures, the woman saint's gendered body embodies not only the variety of female possibility, but also the singularity of individual salvation.

---

[18] In *Forgetful of their Sex: Female Sanctity and Society, ca 500–1100* (Chicago: University of Chicago Press, 1998), Jane Tibbetts Schulenburg discusses this tradition in more detail, pp. 138–39.

[19] *Beowulf*, lines 1056–57, "witig God wyrd forstōde/ and ðæs mannes mōd."

[20] Clare A. Lees, "Engendering Religious Desire: Sex, Knowledge, and Christian Identity in Anglo-Saxon England," *Journal of Medieval and Early Modern Studies* 27:1 (Winter 1997): 35.

Suggestions for Further Reading

Selected primary sources and reference works

Butler, Alban. *Lives of the Saints*. Rev. by Michael J. Walsh. San Francisco: Harper and Row, 1985.

Denomy, Alexander Joseph. *The Old French Lives of Saint Agnes and Other Vernacular Versions of the Middle Ages*. Cambridge: Harvard University Press, 1938.

Farmer, David Hugh. *Oxford Dictionary of Saints*. Oxford: Oxford University Press, 1987.

Lapidge, Michael. *Anglo-Saxon Litanies of the Saints*. London: Henry Bradshaw Society, 1991.

London, British Library, Cotton Julius E.vii. ACLS British Manuscript Project. Shelf no. 041 of *British Museum 3, Aberystwyth*. Microfilm.

Pope, John C., ed. *Homilies of Ælfric: A Supplementary Collection*. London: Oxford University Press, 1967.

Skeat, Walter W., ed. *Ælfric's Lives of Saints*. Early English Text Society Original Series 76, 82, 94, 114. London: Oxford University Press, 1881–1900.

Stevens, Elizabeth, and Pauline Thompson, ed. "Gregory of Ely's Verse Life and Miracles of St Æthelthryth." *Analecta Bollandiana* 106.3–4 (1988): 333–90.

Stevenson, Jane, ed. *Vita Sanctae Mariae Egiptiacae*. In *The Legend of Mary of Egypt in Medieval Insular Hagiography*. Ed. Erich Pope and Bianca Ross. Dublin: Four Courts Press, 1996.

Talbot, Alice-Mary, ed. *Holy Women of Byzantium: Ten Saints' Lives in English Translation*. Byzantine Saints' Lives in Translation 1. Washington, DC: Dumbarton Oaks Center Studies, 1996.

Wormald, Francis, ed. *English Kalendars Before AD 1100*. Henry Bradshaw Society 72. London: Henry Bradshaw Society, 1934.

Selected secondary sources

Atkinson, Clarissa W., ed. *Immaculate and Powerful: The Female in Sacred Image and Social Reality*. Boston: Beacon Press, 1985.

Bell, Rudolf M., and Donald Weinstein. *Saints and Society: The Two Worlds of Western Christendom, 1000–1700*. Chicago: Chicago University Press, 1982.

Bond, Francis. *Dedications & Patron Saints of English Churches: Ecclesiastical Symbolism, Saints and their Emblems*. London: Humphrey Milford, 1914.

Brown, Peter. *The Cult of the Saints: Its Rise and Function in Latin Christianity*. Haskell Lectures on History of Religions. Chicago: University of Chicago Press, 1981.

Brown, Peter. *The Body and Society: Men, Women, and Sexual Renunciation in Early Christianity*. New York: Columbia Press, 1988.

Clark, Elizabeth. *Women in the Early Church*. Wilmington, DE: Glazier, 1983.

Clemoes, Peter, ed. *The Anglo-Saxons: Studies in Some Aspects of their History and Culture Presented to Bruce Dickens*. London: Bowes and Bowes, 1959.

Coon, Lynda L. *Sacred Fictions: Holy Women and Hagiography in Late Antiquity*. Philadelphia: University of Philadelphia Press, 1997.

Cross, J.E. "English Vernacular Saints' Lives Before 1000 A.D." In *Hagiographies, Histoire internationale de la littérature hagiographique, latine et vernaculaire, en Occident des origines à 1550*. Vol. 2. Ed. Guy Philippart. 4 vols. Turnhout: Brepols, 1994–present. Pp. 413–27.

Delehaye, Hippolyte. *The Legends of the Saints: An Introduction to Hagiography*. Trans. V.M. Crawford. London: Longmans, Green and Co., 1907.

Dyas, Dee. *Images of Faith in English Literature 700–1500: An Introduction*. London: Longman, 1997.

Elliott, Alison Goddard. *Roads to Paradise: Reading the Lives of the Early Saints*. Hanover, NH: University Press of New England, 1987.

Erler, Mary, and Maryanne Kowaleski, eds. *Women and Power in the Middle Ages*. Athens, GA: University of Georgia, 1988.

Gneuss, Helmut, "The Origin and Standard Old English at Æthelwold's School at Winchester." *Anglo-Saxon England* 1 (1972): 63–83.

Godden, Malcolm, and Michael Lapidge, eds. *The Cambridge Companion to Old English Literature*. Cambridge: Cambridge University Press, 1991.

Greenfield, Stanley B., and Daniel G. Calder, eds. *A New Critical History of Old English Literature*. New York: New York University Press, 1986.

Gurevich, Aron. *Medieval Popular Culture: Problems of Belief and Perception*. Trans. Janós M. Bak and Paula M. Hollingsworth. Cambridge: Cambridge University Press, 1988.

Heffernan, Thomas J. *Sacred Biography: Saints and their Biographers in the Middle Ages*. Oxford: Oxford University Press, 1988.

Hollis, Stephanie. *Anglo-Saxon Women and the Church: Sharing a Common Fate.* Woodbridge: Boydell Press, 1992.

Huppé, Bernard F., and Paul E. Szarmach, eds. *The Old English Homily and its Backgrounds.* Albany, NY: State University of New York Press, 1978.

John, Eric. *Reassessing Anglo-Saxon England.* Manchester: Manchester University Press, 1996.

Lapidge, Michael. *Anglo-Latin Literature: 600–899.* London: The Hambledon Press, 1996.

Lapidge, Michael. *Anglo-Latin Literature: 900–1066.* London: The Hambledon Press, 1993.

Lees, Clare A. "Engendering Religious Desire: Sex, Knowledge, and Christian Identity in Anglo-Saxon England." *Journal of Medieval and Early Modern Studies* 27:1 (Winter 1997): 16–45.

McNamara, Jo Ann, and Suzanne Fonay Wemple. "Sanctity and Power: The Dual Pursuit of Early Medieval Women." In *Becoming Visible: Women and European History.* 2nd ed. Ed. R. Bridenthal, C. Koonz, and S. Stuard. Boston: Houghton Mifflin, 1987.

Miles, Margaret R. *Carnal Knowing: Female Nakedness and Religious Meaning in the Christian West.* Boston: Beacon, Press, 1989.

Newman, Barbara. *From Virile Woman to WomanChrist.* Studies in Medieval Religion and Literature. Philadelphia: University of Philadelphia Press, 1995.

Olsen, Alexandra Hennessey, " 'De Historiis Sanctorum': A Generic Study of Hagiography." *Genre* 13 (Winter 1980): 407–29.

Petroff, Elizabeth Alvilda. *Body and Soul: Essays on Medieval Women and Mysticism.* Oxford: Oxford University Press, 1994.

Pope, Erich, and Bianca Ross, eds. *The Legend of Mary of Egypt in Medieval Insular Hagiography.* Dublin: Four Courts Press, 1996.

✗ Ridyard, Susan J. *Royal Saints of Anglo-Saxon England: A Study of West Saxon and East Anglian Cults.* Cambridge: Cambridge University Press, 1988.

Robertson, Elizabeth. *Early English Devotional Prose and the Female Audience.* Knoxville: University of Tennessee Press, 1990.

Rollason, David. *Saints and Relics in Anglo-Saxon England.* Oxford: Basil Blackwell, 1989.

Rosenthal, Joel T., ed. *Medieval Women and the Sources of Medieval History.* Athens, GA: University of Georgia Press, 1990.

Salisbury, Joyce. *Church Fathers, Independent Virgins.* London: Verso, 1991.

Scholer, David M., ed. *Women in Early Christianity.* Studies in Early Christianity: A Collection of Scholarly Essays. Ed. Everett Ferguson. New York: Garland, 1993.

Schulenburg, Jane Tibbetts. *Forgetful of their Sex: Female Sanctity and Society, ca 500–1100.* Chicago: University of Chicago Press, 1998.

Sticca, Sandro, ed. *Saints: Studies in Hagiography.* Medieval & Renaissance Texts & Studies 141. Binghamton, NY: State University of New York Press, 1996.

Szarmach, Paul, ed. *Holy Men and Holy Women: Old English Prose Saints' Lives and their Contexts.* Albany, NY: State University of New York Press, 1996.

Townsend, David. "Hagiography." In *Medieval Latin: An Introduction and Bibliographical Guide.* Ed. F.A.C. Montello and A.G. Rigg. Washington, DC: Catholic University of America Press, 1996. Pp. 618–28.

Ward, Benedicta. *Harlots of the Desert: A Study of Repentance in Early Monastic Sources.* Kalamazoo, MI: Cistercian Publications, 1987.

Whatley, E.G. "Late Old English Hagiography, ca. 950–1150." In *Hagiographies, Histoire internationale de la littérature hagiographique, latine et vernaculaire, en Occident des origines à 1550.* Vol. 2. Ed. Guy Philippart. 4 vols. Turnhout: Brepols, 1996. Pp. 429–99.

Wilson, Stephen. *Saints and their Cults: Studies in Religious Sociology, Folklore and History.* Cambridge: Cambridge University Press, 1983.

Wogan-Browne, Jocelyn. "Saints' Lives and the Female Reader." *Forum for Modern Language Studies* 27.4 (October 1991): 314–32.

Index